All True Vows
a memoir

Sharon Downey

WANDERING IN THE WORDS PRESS

Copyright © 2017 Sharon Downey.

All rights reserved. No part of this book may be reproduced, stored in a retrieval system, or transmitted in any form or by any means without the prior written consent of the publisher, except by a reviewer who may quote brief passages in a review to be printed in a newspaper, magazine, blog, or journal.

Visit www.wanderinginthewordspress.com to request permission.

PUBLISHED BY WANDERING IN THE WORDS PRESS

ISBN: 978-0-9991129-6-0

First Edition

This book is a memoir—a story based on memories and feelings, unique to the author.

In these pages, I am not trying to write a history or give an accurate moment-by-moment account of events. My purpose is to share my growth as a human soul with other human souls, in the belief that the connection between each of us strengthens all of us. All of the names in the book, save for those who are deceased, have been changed, along with the name of the organization where I took my vows.

For my parents

Introduction

Sometimes it is better to relinquish a promise than to keep it without heart.
—Sr. Joan Chittister OSB

Our families, in life and in death, help to shape us into who we become. When my father died in 2009, his presence was still palpable in the house he had bought before I was born. He lingered around the edges in the form of brand new socks and underwear still packaged and never used, in a tangle of keys to unknown locks, in dresser drawers full of clippings, pamphlets, and other assorted junk he had collected over a lifetime of squirreling away things "in case I need it later." His continual need to save, stash, and hide came slamming up against my mother's need to sort, clean, and purge. I walked into the master bedroom to find her dumping a drawer full of ephemera into a white trash bag. She hadn't even glanced at the drawer's contents. "What a packrat," she mumbled. "What the hell was he saving all of this junk for?"

Two years later, as I stood in the same room and sifted through her belongings, I shook my head. "You have no room to talk," I muttered to her spirit. I could still sense her here, in the house where we had lived my entire life. I dug through her closet to find brand new clothes, some with the price tags still attached, saved for a special occasion that never came. There were the dishes from her first disastrous marriage, still packed carefully in their original box, and mementos from my brother's and my childhoods, including baby teeth in a cracked, used prescription bottle. It was like an archeological dig. Evidently her need to clear away things she viewed as useless didn't extend to her own possessions. I uncovered a shoebox filled with old photographs, and though I had a house full of items to clear away, I couldn't resist going through them. The box was a portal to the past. I held in my hands the faces of those long gone.

In one tiny photograph, a group of four women clustered together, one dressed in nun garb, the others, elderly, in simple housedresses, all with the same facial features. These women were my grandmother and her sisters, my father's mother and aunts. My father's mother's family came to America from Ireland. In classic Irish-American style, my great-grandparents had numerous children, and the expectation was that one or more would go to the church to serve god as priests or nuns. My great-aunt Bridget Irene went on to become Sister Mary Inviolata. In the photograph, she stands behind my seated paternal grandmother, her head covered with a white wimple and long black veil, a small, secretive smile on her broad face. I learned about my father's family from my mother, the bits and pieces she had gleaned not so much from my father, but from his brothers and other family members.

Sr. Inviolata was buried in the same cemetery as my parents. The nuns of her order, the Sisters of Charity, were in a separate section of the grounds. Sr. Inviolata's resting spot was marked with a plain white marble headstone. The sisters were laid to rest in neat lines, much as they had sat together in their order in the motherhouse chapel to say their prayers. While some of the nuns' markers bore their last names, my great aunt's stone simply read Sr. Mary Inviolata, along with the years of her birth and death. It was as if she'd had no family, no life before she took this strange name. Inviolata comes from the word "inviolate," that which is undisturbed, unbroken. Did she choose this name herself or did someone choose it for her? Did it refer to the untouched virginity attributed to the Virgin Mary? I had been unable to ask these questions when I met Sr. Inviolata for the first and only time, when I was a toddler.

Once over breakfast, my mother, a wonderful storyteller, told me the tale, the one I had a starring role in, about visiting Sr. Inviolata. "I didn't want to go to see her, but that didn't matter. Your *other* grandmother always got her way." This was Mom's way of denoting it was my father's mother, her dreaded mother-in-law, not her own mother, whom she was talking about. Mom was convinced that Josephine Kirby Downey had not liked her. My mother perceived that her mother-in-law felt that my father had married beneath himself by taking a woman who had been divorced and a "dumb hunky"—in my mother's words—to boot. Mom put more sugar in her coffee and stirred it vigorously. "All the way out to Baden. It was so hot." I sipped my own cup.

The journey took place the summer before my brother was born, 1963. Mom was probably five months pregnant at the time. She had told me so often how being pregnant with my brother had been very difficult. He weighed over nine pounds at birth. I pictured an uncomfortable, hot, and hormonal woman with a squirming toddler— I would have been just over two years old—making the trip in a car without air conditioning to visit a convent which, in truth, was only a half hour away from home. A small town, Baden, Pennsylvania, with its decaying steel mills and an abandoned railway yard, was one more spot in the dying rust belt.

My mother's past history with nuns, those who had taught her in primary school, wasn't very good. No, that's an understatement. It was horrible. Nuns cracked rulers against knuckles for the slightest infraction. A teacher slapped my mother's sister across the ear so hard that it bled. When my mother was in the fourth grade, a nun assigned to teach math simply allowed the class to read storybooks rather than attempt to teach a subject she herself didn't fully understand. The whole experience was the reason why my brother and I ended up attending public school. No wonder my mother didn't want to make that trip.

"It was some kind of holiday or special day for your great aunt, so she could see people." Mom gulped her coffee down, draining the cup. She drank coffee like most people drink cold water when they are thirsty. "Your father and his brothers would go visit her, and she was behind a grille, so they couldn't see her. Sister Inviolata took you from me and went behind the lattice-work screen in the chapel. We couldn't go with her, but she could take you—evidently. She went and stood in front of the crucifix and pointed to it. Then she walked over to the statute of St. Joseph and did the same thing. Then she went over to the Blessed Virgin Mary. You started waving your hands at the statue and babbling away. She brings you back to me and tells me you're going to be a nun. I grabbed you back out of her hands so fast and told her 'over my dead body.' Dad tried to calm me down, but I was so mad! Who was she to have you locked up like all of them? Just because you liked one statue more than another! Ridiculous." Mom pursed her lips and shoved away the cup and saucer, the anger from all those years ago flaring in her eyes.

I sat there drinking my coffee slowly, seeing in my mind's eye a red-haired, curly headed little girl wearing a summer sundress, held in the arms of a black-clad figure. The girl paid little if any attention to the crucifix, the dark brown figure on the black wood holding no interest for her. St. Joseph was somber, holding a little baby in his right arm, a sheaf of lilies in his left. He was dressed in browns and dark greens, with the little boy held out and away from his body—well, that was nice, but not very exciting. But the Lady! Oh, how lovely! Blue dress and white veil, in a niche decorated with blue tiles all around her and stars made of gold sprinkled about… She held her little boy the way a good momma should, nice and tight, and she was smiling at him. He must be a very good boy. Of course, the little girl wanted to touch her. The Lady reminded her of the statue her Baba had on the dresser at home, only the statue didn't have a baby, and the little girl wanted Baba's Lady to have one, a little girl.

A little girl just like me.

So there you have three reactions to the same event: one seeing it as prophetic, one viewing it in horror, and one who wanted what she wanted because she was twenty-eight months old and she didn't yet understand that life doesn't always work that way.

I picked up the dishes from the table and moved to the sink. I had been a Franciscan nun for fifteen years and had made the decision not to renew my vows. "I guess she was right," my mother said. I turned back to her sitting there at the table. When I was child, my mother had always seemed big to me—tall, heavy, stalwart—a presence that had filled my world. She was then older, not quite seventy-five, smaller, frailer, yet her hazel eyes still held fire. When I looked at her, I saw her mother, my Baba, the same firm chin, the same large, strong hands capable of so much. I paused and dropped the door on the dishwasher.

"You're giving her more credit than I think she's due." I put the dishes into the machine. "She meant that I would be like her, vowed for life. I quit, remember?"

Mom nodded her head. "I'm glad you realized that it wasn't for you. I always knew it wasn't, but no one listens to their mother."

I leaned over and kissed her on the forehead. "No, not always. But the only way you learn is by making mistakes, right?"

All the True Vows
are secret vows
the ones we speak out loud
are the ones we break.

—David Whyte

First Vow — Age 16

My childhood home in Pittsburgh, Pennsylvania, was a tiny, three-bedroom house perched on the side of a hill. When I was almost three years old, my mother gave birth to my younger brother, Norm. Born the week before Christmas, he arrived home wrapped in a Christmas stocking. To my young mind, he was a gift for me, a baby doll if you will. I found out quickly that this doll cried lustily, and everyone fussed over him. My earliest memory of him is seeing my mother seated in the rocking chair desperately trying to lull him to sleep. I stood in front her, furious. The little usurper had taken *my* place on my mother's lap. My mother recounted to me later how I had turned my back on her, grabbed my teddy bear, and stomped up the stairs. "You never asked to be rocked again," my mother related to me with a smile.

After my brother was born, he took over the smallest bedroom, and I moved in to sleep with my grandmother, my mother's mother, in her ancient double bed with a mattress that dipped into a well in the center. Both of my parents grew up in households where there wasn't enough room; sharing a bed with another family member was common, so they didn't give this arrangement much thought. Above the bed on the wall was the crucifix, the happy death cross. Beneath the brass corpus, the cross came apart, the top covering an opening where a flask of holy water, a candle, and a prayer book nestled inside. This was in case you had to call the priest to give someone the last rites, evidence of my grandmother's belief that it was good to be prepared for any eventuality. It was a reminder of death, the silent and unbidden visitor that my grandmother had met with many times in her life, first with some of her children, and then her husband, my grandfather.

Every night before going to sleep, no matter how tired she may have been, my grandmother, or Baba as we called her, said the entire rosary, all 150 Hail Marys. On the dresser next to our bed stood her two-foot-tall stone statue of the Blessed Mother. Mary was dressed in a blue gown, a white veil covering her head, her curling brown hair just edging out from underneath it. Her face and eyes were downcast, and her hands lay crossed on her breast, just below her flaming heart. Her legs beneath her skirts were contrapposto, as if she were about to step off the base she was standing on and come to the rescue. My grandmother trusted in Mary completely, certain that her intercession was what would keep all of us safe and would allow her husband, my grandfather, to spend less time in the fires of purgatory and gain heaven a bit quicker. God, after all, had the whole world to deal with, but Mary always had time for those who asked for her help.

My Baba died when I was ten years old. Her loss was a pivot point in my life. One of the pillars that had held up the world for me was gone. Both of my parents worked, sometimes at odd hours. My Baba took care of my brother and me, feeding us, dressing us, while also taking care of the housework. She was my second mother, on whose broad lap I could nestle and feel safe. She helped my mother get us off to school and was there to offer delicious homemade treats and a warm, loving embrace when we came home. My mother too felt keenly the loss of her mother, and so the time after my Baba's passing was one of deep sadness as my mother struggled to regain her footing in the world. Suddenly, I had that double bed to myself, the happy death cross still above my head as I slept and the statue of Mary still keeping vigil over me on the dresser.

***

Six years later, during the summer of 1977, came another turning point in my life. My father came home one evening from his job on the railroad, sick as a dog, as my mother would recall it years later. My father had spent the day hiding out from his boss in the welding shack because he was unable to work due to the pain and nausea he felt, but to leave and go home would mean a day without pay. By the end of the day, his face held a sickly green tinge. He complained of crushing pain in his chest and left arm. He refused to eat supper and headed upstairs to the bathroom. My mother pleaded with him to go to a doctor or to the hospital, but he refused. His face turned ashen, and he was covered in sweat. Throughout the night, he vomited repeatedly into a bucket my mother placed next to his bed. The following morning, my father dragged himself to the bathroom, took a shower, dressed, and drove himself and the entire family to the emergency room of the local hospital. (Yes, I think you can safely say insanity runs in my family.) The hospital immediately admitted him, and the doctors were astonished that he was still alive. He'd had a massive heart attack, and there was a lot of doubt as to whether or not his heart could recover.

Our family doctor conveyed the bad news to my mother, my brother, and me in the waiting area in the emergency room. I sat, frozen, unable to process the information. When you are sixteen years old, you are at a stage in your life when everything and everyone around you has to stay the same so that you can be the only point of change in the universe. It's a time when you can be completely selfish, narcissistic, and painfully shortsighted. My first thought was how grateful I was that this was not happening to my mother. It's hard for me to realize that and write this now. If one of my two parents were going to die, I did not want it to be my mother. We would argue and we had our issues like any mother and daughter, but her demonstrative love was my anchor. My father's coldness and inability to express his emotions was a thin soup compared to my mother's full expression of her emotions, both of love and of anger. You never had to worry where you stood with my mother—she was always upfront with her feelings.

One of the photographs of my early childhood tells the story of my relationship with my father. My mother snapped the photo when I was just under a year old. Dressed in a dark green velvet dress for the Christmas holidays, I sit in a tiny wooden rocking chair. My burnished red hair is in little spiky curls all over my head. My gray-blue eyes and milky white face hold a stunned and blank expression. Crouching beside me on one knee is my father, his hair and eye color a match for my own. His right hand clasps his left wrist, and he smiles broadly for the camera. He is not looking at me or reaching out to touch me. He's not holding me or attempting to comfort me from the obvious fear I have of the camera. It's as if two strangers posed with one another, capturing a moment before moving on with their separate lives.

My mother brought the photo to work to show some of her coworkers. She told me that her supervisor, who walked up later to the group, asked, "Why did you take a picture of your husband with a baby doll?"

"That's my daughter!" my mother retorted. The man mumbled an apology and walked off. But that story made sense to me. In a way, it was as if my father was posing with any treasured inanimate object, like a new car. You don't hug the car—well, most people don't—but you stand proudly next to it, showing it off. But I was a child, not a plaything that could be displayed and later packed away.

I often wondered why my mother never called my dad by his given name; she always referred to him as "Dad," even in public around total strangers. I finally asked her about it. "Well, I had to make sure you kids knew who he was. You know he never talks very much." I laughed at this explanation, but the fact she felt this was necessary troubled me. My father viewed his role as the breadwinner; his job was to provide the necessities of life, and my mother's job was to take care of everything else. He communicated to his children through his wife—"What's she going to do?" was a favorite question, even right in front of me. As I grew older, this go-between relationship infuriated me. "I'm right here, you know," I'd burst out. "Ask me!" That would only drive him deeper into silence. It was as if a wall went up between my father and me very early in my life that was too high for me to climb over. I don't know who built the wall. Did we work on it together? I suppose we did, but as I grew up, I simply stopped trying to scale it.

My relationship with my mother presents itself in a different old photograph. In it, my mother holds my brother and me on her spacious lap. I am somewhere between three and four years old, my brother just over a year old. My brother is reclining slightly and looking off to the right, not paying attention to the camera. I'm giggling, my face full of glee, something filling me with mischievous delight. My mother's face is turned toward me, an expression of distaste curling the corners of her mouth. I'm not cooperating, not doing what she expects of me in that moment. I should have faced forward, sat still, looked at the camera and smiled sweetly. Instead, here was this devilish little girl on her lap, ruining the photo. My mother's world was about control, about keeping order, because to reduce the chaos that was a constant threat, to "make things just so," as she frequently stated, was how she kept her fears at bay.

As I grew older, I realized that my parents were locked in a struggle between my father's reticence and my mother's need for control. Ours was not a quiet, easy household. The steadiness and imperturbability of my father regressed into stubbornness and intractability. My mother's nurturance morphed into smothering and neediness. As the oldest child and the dutiful daughter, it was my job to smooth things over. I could not reach my father, so I spent my time consoling my mother, moving from child to friend in ways that were not healthy for either of us. I wanted her love—in fact, I craved it—so I would go along with her, doing her bidding, be the amenable child, but only to a point. I always held something back. Some part of myself stopped my soul's complete annihilation. The more she wanted the boundaries between us to be completely porous, the more she wanted my inner life revealed, the cleverer I became at hiding it.

My relationship with my younger brother was much more straightforward. I tried to be the bossy older sister, and he rebelled against that with his own brand of feistiness and a great ability to ignore me. What kept my brother and me close was our us-versus-them mentality. When we would squabble, our mother often said, "All you have is each other." Her words worked. Norm and I learned to work together to get what we wanted—for the most part. We did have our moments of sibling rivalry—the usual fights for space in the back seat of the car. *He's touching me!*

Much later in my life, in a conversation with James Wells, a tarot consultant based in Ontario, I talked about the pain of my family lineage, and how woundedness had made its way through the generations. My parents were children of the Depression and of immigrants, who struggled to make it in the strange, new world of America. My paternal grandmother took in boarders to make ends meet. Strangers moved in and out of my father's childhood home, and I was certain the disruption and lack of privacy only contributed to my father's secretive nature and his need for concealment and privacy. My mother told me of standing on the sidewalk, clutching her mother's purse, while her family's belongings were loaded into a truck, their home lost to foreclosure. Displacement, loss, and death were the common threads of my parents' lives and had helped to make them the people they were.

Now, with Death sitting down and taking up a great deal of space, we shunted aside all of those family dynamics. While my response to my father's illness was shock and numbness, my mother went into full panic mode. She believed fully that my father was going to die, leaving her with two teenagers, a mortgage, and only a tenth-grade education to find a job with which to support us. Life insurance was non-existent; my father foolishly believed he could not afford it. My mother took steps to establish some sense of control over the situation. She emptied all of our meager savings, including tiny accounts that my parents held for my brother and me. She contacted the railroad about sick pay and called all of her creditors, telling them what had happened, so she could find out how best she could avoid being turned over to a collection agency.

Looking back, I have a sense of admiration for my mother; she was trying her best to cope with a very difficult situation. To make matters worse, she didn't know how to drive, and though I was sixteen, my father had refused to allow me to learn because he would have had the additional burden of insuring me. We were dependent on the kindness of my uncles, my father's brothers, none of whom my mother liked very much, to ferry us around.

I felt useless in the midst of the chaos that surrounded me, a feeling I've never handled very well. My response to any crisis is to do something, even if it's unnecessary, like cleaning out a closet or making endless to-do lists. My middle name should have been "control freak." That evening, sitting on the edge of my bed, where my beloved Baba had recited her nightly rosary, I worried and fretted, looking for a way to contribute. I decided that while I couldn't drive us back and forth from the hospital or earn enough money to keep us from losing our home, I could pray as my grandmother had always done. I found an old prayer book, a tiny white missal that my mother had from her first marriage. In it were beautiful litanies to the Virgin. I lit a candle surreptitiously—my mother did not like to have candles lit, fearing the house burning down—and I knelt before the statue of Mary. I read in a faint whisper the titles of the Virgin: Mystical Rose, Tower of Ivory, House of Gold, Morning Star. I glanced up at the statue, seeing her secret smile as a benediction.

Despite the feeling that I had Mary on my side, I knew I had to make a bargain. The god I knew from my youth was one who wanted and demanded sacrifice. The bible showed this repeatedly, from clear back to the Old Testament, with Abraham ready and willing to slice his son Isaac open, all the way to Jesus dying on a cross. You had to give up something, sacrifice something, to receive something. The idea came from my own childhood, even from the current crisis my family was in. My father had sacrificed himself by staying at work while desperately ill so that we could have money for food and shelter. You gave up what you most wanted, set aside your own feelings and desires, for the good of others. I looked up at the Lady, and the plan arose fully formed, an idea to this day I have no idea where it came from. "I'll give you my virginity to keep safe. I promise to never marry and never love anyone in a physical way in return for my father's life," I whispered to god. Of course, now this makes little sense. Why would god care about my intact hymen? But I had before me the epitome of virginal purity, one who the Church claimed had lived chastely her whole life and who had given birth without one breath of pain. If she was his son's mother, he must place value on that.

I prayed and made an offering of something about which I had yet to be tested. I was sixteen and barely ninety-eight pounds soaking wet. I had a flat chest, crooked teeth, wild hair, and an extreme shyness. I had no concerns that I couldn't keep my vow. All I had to worry about was god keeping his end of the bargain.

When I awoke the next day, I opened my eyes and looked up at the statue on the dresser. For a split second, through a trick of the light, my own wishful imagination, or perhaps in reality, the statue's hands parted and one extended itself outward towards me, in a gesture of blessing. Mary was in my corner. My prayer was answered. My father made a slow but steady recovery, and in about three months, he returned to work. Our family life went on much as before. I never spoke to anyone about my vow, or of how the statue of Mary blessed me that morning long ago.

Sharon Downey

The Sinner's Prayer

When I was a young child, Mr. Urban, an insurance salesman who attended the same church as Baba, would come to our house to visit with her. The only word picture I can offer about him is "Dracula in a business suit." He wore his dyed coal-black hair slicked back. His suits were meticulous, and he sported a pinky ring on his right hand. My mother could barely hide her obvious distaste at his appearance and overly courtly manners, but my grandmother lapped it right up. Baba bought a policy from Mr. Urban for my brother. The policy paid the settlement if my brother died or when he turned eighteen to help him pay for college. There was no such policy purchased for me.

When I asked my mother about this years later, after she brought up Mr. Urban in one of her I-remember-when stories, she paused.

"Well, Mr. Urban said that girls didn't need money for school; they get married and have kids." She lowered her head under my laser glare.

"And you believed him?" I asked, my mouth agape.

"Your grandmother was buying the policy, not me," she said. "We didn't have the money for such foolishness. Besides, your brother got nothing. The premiums went unpaid after she died, and the policy on him was canceled."

The prediction of Mr. Urban about females not attending college did come true for me, at least in part. I graduated from high school in 1979, and I had convinced myself that college was a dream only other people could have. I put myself through a nine-month business school course and got a job at a local bank doing data entry. It was mind-numbing, repetitive work. The petty gossip and rumors that swept through the office made me feel like I was back in high school. I kept to myself, following the work ethic I had learned from my parents: keep your head down, follow the rules, don't make waves, and hold onto your job—no matter what. As children of the Great Depression and victims of repeated plant closures and company moves, my parents had taught me to cling to a job with both hands, both feet, and using your teeth if necessary. It was the early 1980s and Reaganomics was in full swing. Everywhere you looked, people were losing their jobs, companies were folding, and money was tight. I was fortunate, my parents told me repeatedly. Dreams were just that—dreams—useless things that put nothing in your pocket. Raised in the complex stew of fear, scarcity, and lack, I closed my eyes to whatever my heart wanted and held on tight to what I had.

In 1986, I met Grace. She was tall and thin, with curling black hair and a huge bright smile. I remember her coming into the workroom where I sat one afternoon. On the side table was an open bag of potato chips. She looked at the bag longingly. One of my coworkers told her to help herself. "No, I just want to smell them," Grace said, lifting the edge of the bag delicately and sniffing the odor of grease and salted potatoes emanating from within. "I'm fasting," she went on. She put the bag down, smiled, and left the room. A chorus of giggles, hoots, and murmurs ensued. *Who does she think she is?* I was puzzled. It was September. No church calendar that I knew of made fasting mandatory at that time of the year. Was she fasting for a medical reason?

I finally got up the nerve to ask Grace about the fasting. "I'm in my church's Franciscan order. We call it Chapter," she explained. "We fast on Wednesdays from all solid food, until we meet together. Then we have supper and break the fast."

"But you're married!" I said. The religious I knew were unmarried nuns and priests.

"Oh, we have married people, divorced people, and single people. It doesn't matter. God calls who he wants to a vowed life." She reached into her shirt and pulled out a medal that hung from a silver chain. It was shaped like the head of Christ wearing a crown of thorns, his mouth open in agony. "This is called an Ecce Homo medal. It's my engagement ring. In three years, I'll be the Bride of Christ and get a gold wedding ring to wear on my right hand." She tucked the medal back down inside her clothes. The ease with which Grace conveyed all of this information astonished me. I could never imagine sharing such intimate details of my private life with anyone in the office. Grace told me that Christians were to be the perfume that pervaded every corner of life, bringing with them the sweetness of Christ and his love for everyone. She told me about her husband, a mean drunk whom she had learned to ignore as much as possible, and about her grown children, two daughters and a son. Grace drew people to her, even those who laughed at her behind her back, and she talked to everyone, treating them all the same, with a smile and much laughter. Her ability to be comfortable in every situation made me both envious and grateful. Whatever it was that made Grace be Grace—well, I wanted it. Nowadays, Grace would have been my girl crush.

A frequent topic of Grace's was the need for a born-again experience. "Everyone is a sinner; we're all in the same boat," she explained. "We all need Jesus to come into our hearts and give us a second chance." This thinking was very different from what I had learned in catechism class in the Catholic Church. You went to confession, mass, and communion. You took the sacraments. And if you were good, you went to heaven. If not so good, you were off to purgatory for a "time out." By virtue of birth, you were in "the club." There was no formula to follow; you didn't have to convert or be born again.

There are times when you have to take a long, hard look at your life and figure out where it's going. As far as I could see, mine was going nowhere. I went to work at a soul-crushing, monotonous job, I came home to the same family dynamic I had lived in my entire life. I was treading water. No one else in my family, particularly my parents, thought this was bad or unusual. On both sides of the family tree were women who never married, either by choice or for religious reasons. If you were unmarried, you stayed home with your family; it was where you belonged. After my mother's first marriage ended in divorce, she promptly returned to live with her mother, and when she married my father, she brought her mother along into the marriage. It was what you did. Even my brother remained living at home until he married.

Unhappy as I was with my life and the way it was heading, I thought it wouldn't hurt to give Grace's way a try. I reasoned I wouldn't have to say anything to anyone; it would just be between god and me. At mass on the Sunday after Easter, when I came back to our pew after receiving communion, I knelt down for a few moments of quiet reflection. The host was stuck to the roof of my mouth as usual, and I worked with my tongue to unglue it and swallow. I didn't know the formula for the "Sinner's Prayer," so I just spoke from the heart, inside my thoughts. "I can't go on like I am. I'm not happy. I'm sorry if you're mad at me. I just want what Grace has. Please." I managed to get the host unstuck, and it slid down my throat. Then something odd happened. I felt—lighter—as if a huge weight was off my back. I straightened my shoulders and looked around me. Nothing else was different—same people in the pews, my mother beside me, the light pouring in through the stained-glass windows, the lilies around the statue of the risen Christ, the organ playing softly in the background. Something had happened to me, inside my soul. But what it was, I wasn't exactly sure.

Looking back in that moment, I now know the universe was giving me an opportunity—to take action in my life, to turn the course of it around. I received a get-out-of jail-free card, a do-over if you will. I could have decided to quit working and go back to school or find another job or move to the other side of the country. I could have stayed right where I was, but with a newfound sense of freedom and purpose. Instead of taking that gift and making the most of it, I turned the card back in and set off to find a new set of shackles to replace the ones I had just removed.

All True Vows

First Prayer Meeting

I found myself spending more time hanging around Grace's desk at work. Her easy manner with everyone, cracking jokes and listening to all of the sad stories anyone had to tell, fascinated me and made my little introverted heart jealous. As our friendship grew, she asked me if I would like to come with her to her church for a prayer meeting. The prayer meetings were held on Monday nights at eight. St. Xavier's Chapel was located in the Mon Valley, about forty-five minutes from my home. But it may as well have been a thousand miles away. Although I had finally paid for someone to teach me to drive in my early twenties (my father's attempts to teach me in my teens had been a complete disaster), I didn't own a car, and my father was adamant that I would never drive his. I rode the bus each day into town to go to work.

I told Grace that while I would like to come to her church I had no means of getting there. Grace, however, never took no for the final answer to any situation. There was always a way to get what you wanted, particularly if god was involved. If god wanted me there, then god would make a way. "Could your father bring you as far as the Cogo's convenience store on Route 51? That's at the bottom of the hill where I live. Annie and I can meet you there." Annie was Grace's closest friend. They were both members of the church's Chapter and had known each other for years.

The next hurdle was scraping up the courage to ask my father for the ride. I knew this was going to be difficult. Asking my parents for anything, particularly my father, was excruciating. The go-to answer was always a resounding no. It led me to just stop asking rather than ask and be turned down again. But sometimes the desire for a certain object, usually tied to my childlike need to fit in and be like everyone else, overcame that block. I remember I wanted a new blouse to wear to perform in a choral concert in eighth grade. All of the girls had to wear white blouses and long, dark skirts. I had a blouse, but it was fussy, with a big bow in front, the fabric stiff and scratchy, and I hated it. I saw what the other girls were wearing—soft satiny blouses with pin tucks at the shoulders. I convinced my mother that a new blouse was in order. So we went shopping, all four of us, because we needed my father to drive and my mother to do the shopping, me to try the blouse on, and my brother—well, my mother wasn't leaving him home alone. We went from store to store. The blouses either didn't fit, didn't come in white, or were just as ugly as the one I already owned. My father grew more and more angry. Finally, he blew up. "What's wrong with the one you have?"

I ducked my head.

My mother, for once, didn't come to my defense.

"Do you want or need a new blouse? Which is it?" he steamrolled on.

"I...I...want a new one." My face flushed with shame and yes, anger.

"Well, if you don't need it, what the hell are we doing here?" He stomped out of the store, the rest of us trailing after him. In my father's world, there were needs—a full stomach, a roof over your head, a car to get back and forth to work to provide the two previous examples—and there were wants, which the world seldom filled, and certainly, no one should ever ask for, because life didn't work like that. Asking for a ride to go to a church that my father didn't attend was definitely a want.

I screwed up my courage and asked for the ride, saying Grace had invited me and I didn't want to hurt her feelings by not going. Yes, I was a budding con artist. And unbelievably, it worked. My mother expressed her reservations, loudly, as was her way. "You have a religion, you know." She fumed as she got ready to go with my father and me that Monday night. I wasn't sure why she was going, until it dawned on me that she wanted to see the "crazies," as she called Grace and Annie. But why did I want to go? Because I had been invited? Because I was looking for something? Or was I living out some delayed adolescent rebellion? Honestly, it was the last choice. I had been Miss Goody Two-Shoes my entire life. I had never challenged my parents on anything. They always knew where I was and what I was up to—mostly because I was on their living room couch reading a book. Now I was off to dabble in some "strange" religion. No wonder my mother was freaking out.

When my parents and I arrived at the Cogo's, a beat-up Chevy Chevette pulled into the lot after us. Annie's car was a rolling wreck and looked as if it had about a million miles on it, which probably wasn't far from the truth. I thanked my parents for bringing me, and my mother just shook her head, her eyes glued to the Chevette, trying to see the occupants inside. My father's only comment: "Watch she doesn't kill you in that thing."

I climbed into the back seat with Grace's daughter and granddaughter. The little girl didn't have a car seat; I'm not sure if they were required back then or if we were violating the law. The car didn't have air conditioning, and Annie was a smoker, so we barreled our way down Route 51 with the windows wide open. I perched on the outer edge of the uncomfortable back seat feeling the hot air rush past my face.

Grace sat up in front with Annie and chattered the whole way out to the church. "Now, when we get there," she said, "Annie, Marie, and I have to go upstairs and say hello to the Lord before we can talk to anybody, but we'll be right down. You can just sit downstairs and wait for us." After about a half hour or so, we arrived at a gravel road that led up to a small wooden frame and concrete block structure.

"This is it," Annie said, pulling into a gravel-lined parking lot. The door to the basement of the building was open. As the rest of the group trooped up the stairs to the first floor, I hesitated in the doorway before stepping inside. In front of me, at the back of the room, sat a man dressed all in black. He was thin, angular, with long legs crossed at the ankle in front of him. He wore Teva sandals on his bare feet and a crucifix on a silver chain around his neck. He focused on a book he held in his hands, glasses perched on his hawk-like nose. His hair was close cropped, flecked with grey. He was tan, but not overly so. He made no effort to take notice of me. I assumed he was absorbed in his reading, so I took a seat in a chair nearest the doorway where a little bit of air was coming in, but certainly not enough to quell the heat.

The group returned, and Marie's daughter toddled over to the man. He made a fuss over her, calling her baby and giving her kisses on her face and hands. Each of the women greeted him in turn, exchanging hugs and kisses. Grace finally pointed in my direction and introduced me. "This is Sharon; she's my friend from work. This is Father Thomas," she said, turning to me. I rose from my seat and walked over. A cold pair of gray eyes met mine, and the heat of his smile did not warm them one bit. They were the eyes of a predator sizing up its prey. Despite the warmth of the summer evening, I shivered. He extended a well-groomed hand and shook mine.

"Welcome, welcome," he said. He commanded Annie to see if I wanted some coffee. We all lingered in the basement, until Fr. Thomas announced it was time to go upstairs. A few more people had joined the group, and I could hear guitar music coming from the floor above. The chapel itself was small, with about twelve wooden pews, six on each side of a short center aisle. At the front of the room was the altar, and hanging on the wood paneled wall behind it was a large, floor-to-ceiling wooden crucifix. The back and side doors were left open to let in air.

Fr. Thomas sat in a chair facing the congregation. A woman, who I later learned was his wife, Lena, sat to his right and played the guitar. A few people clustered around her, singing loudly and rather off key. The singing continued for a bit, and then Fr. Thomas led us in prayers of praise and prayers of petition, punctuated by more singing.

Then the service took a strange turn. Fr. Thomas started saying things like, "Someone here came tonight with a stomach ache. The Lord is healing you right now. Praise you, Jesus!" Affirmative murmurs and calls of "Thank you, Lord!" were uttered around the room. I didn't know what to make of it. How did he know what was going on in someone else's stomach? Fr. Thomas announced a financial blessing for someone else. Then he spoke the words that went straight to my heart: "Someone here is burdened with loneliness tonight, and god wants to heal you from that." I knew immediately, beyond any doubt, that that someone was me. I felt a white-hot burning sensation in my gut. I burst into tears. Grace leaned over and wrapped her arm around my shoulders, shushing me like a child. I was at once both ashamed and scared, unsure of what had just happened to me. Leaning into Grace, I pulled tissues from my purse and wiped my eyes, embarrassed at my behavior. It seemed that no one took notice or offense at my reaction; in this place, it evidently was the norm for people to break down and cry.

Then Fr. Thomas called for anyone who wanted a fresh infilling of the Holy Spirit to come forward and he would pray with them. People rose up, one by one, and sat in the pew in front of him. He placed his hands on their heads, leaning in so that he and the person before him were touching, forehead to forehead. Some sat before him for only a moment; others appeared to be getting a lecture from him. All the while, the music continued, the choir—if you could call it that—sang to drown out the conversation in the front of the church. When the last person who had come up for prayer sat back down, the first half of the prayer meeting ended with more singing and praise.

Everyone trooped back downstairs, where we had "fellowship," along with coffee and cookies. I sat with Grace, observing the others around me. Grace pointed at the crowd, naming the people seated nearest to us. There was Marge, who lived only a short walk from the church, with her bipolar son, Greg. Pat, an elderly woman with a slightly askew wig, sat with her sister drinking coffee. Grace's niece, Cathy, sat talking with Fr. Thomas, her head bobbing up and down in agreement to his words. I didn't ask Grace any questions about what had happened to me upstairs. I told myself we could talk about it later, on the ride home.

The second half of the meeting was the preaching portion of the service. When it was over, we left the building. Fr. Thomas came and stood in the doorway, calling to Grace. She walked back to him and then turned to call me over to them. Fr. Thomas spoke to me, his voice stern. "That healing for loneliness was for you. This is your home now. Grace, give her my phone number. You can call anytime." I dumbly nodded my head, not sure what I was supposed to say to this. If the "healing" was from god, was it appropriate to thank Thomas? What did he mean that this was now my home?

All of us got into the car, and we drove off. Grace was delighted at what Fr. Thomas had said to me. She warbled all the way home "Aren't you glad you came? God is so good, isn't he? You just never know what he's going to do or how he's going to move. That's why I hate to miss out on anything at church."

At that moment, I realized that I was happy—more than happy, I was elated. I had been singled out—me, who never was chosen for anything. I was still that little girl in the photo, sitting beside the man who didn't know how to be a father to her. I wanted that specialness, that proof of love to keep coming. I was like an addict after her first high; I just wanted more of the same, score another hit. The elation fizzled out in a flash under the scathing white-hot anger of my mother, who could barely contain herself as I got into my father's car. "It's late. You have to be at work tomorrow, how are you going to get up in the morning?" Before I could reply, the next salvo was primed and ready, and she aimed this one right at my heart. "I suppose they signed you up already. You're probably going to go live with that nutty friend of yours and be off singing 'Kumbaya' every night." Translation: *You will go off and leave me alone with your father.*

"I didn't...I didn't sign anything."

My father was no help of course. He was just looking to keep out of the line of fire himself, but I knew he agreed with her. Different was bad, just plain dangerous in his book, and this whole experiment in religion was different and therefore no good.

"Well?" she asked, turning around to look at me in the back seat. "Are you going to tell us what happened or not?"

My usual reticence and basic good sense flew out the window. I did about the dumbest thing I had ever done up to that point. I told her what Fr. Thomas had said to me during the prayer meeting. "Well, that's it then," my mother said, turning around to face the front. "We've lost you. You belong to them now." What she meant was that she had lost me, her friend, her confidant, her solace in the loneliness that was her home and her marriage. The rest of the ride home was in silence. Any joy I had felt slipped away like air from a leaking balloon.

I didn't know it at the time, but the church was having a membership drive, trying to "bring souls into the kingdom." I was, in essence, a big catch. A young woman with a paying job and no husband or children. I was ripe for picking. I feel certain that Grace told Fr. Thomas all about me—the shy young girl who lived at home, no attachments, no life of her own. How easy it would have been for him to translate that information into the blessing he pronounced for me. I was an innocent, taken advantage of, and I participated in it fully. That night started my journey down the rabbit hole that was my vowed life.

Sharon Downey

The CRC and "the Bishop"

I sat in front of the television, mesmerized by a woman with elven features. She was dressed in a long flowing gossamer gown, waving her arms in exuberance. "The Holy Spirit does the work," she said in sibilant speech, her S's stretching out, snakelike. The black and white set prohibited me from seeing what I knew from magazine photos were the soft aqua color of her gown and the bright auburn of her curly hair. She went on talking about healing and gifts of the Spirit, smiling beatifically into the camera.

Then my mother entered the room. It was Sunday morning, and my brother and I were supposed to be on our way to catechism class. We attended a public elementary school, and so religious training for us was on Sunday mornings. My brother was usually the one guilty of putting the brakes on, slowing down our getting ready by whining and what my mother labeled as "putzing." Instead, here was her normally compliant older child staring at the television set. Worse yet, I was watching...

"Shut that off." She snapped the switch herself. "That woman is a witch. Go get dressed!" I slunk off to my room, wondering why my mother had called the woman with a lisp a witch.

The witch, as it turned out, was instrumental in the spiritual life of "the Bishop," the man who founded the Church of the Resurrected Christ, where I would eventually take my Franciscan vows. During one of Kathryn Kuhlman's services at the First Presbyterian Church in downtown Pittsburgh, she announced that there was someone in the balcony having a "Paul experience," a direct encounter with Christ that led to conversion and an infilling of the Holy Spirit. "The Bishop," who at that time was a factory worker, would claim that experience and change not only his own life, but also hundreds of other lives, including mine.

The Church of the Resurrected Christ, or CRC, had at its core the evangelistic preaching of what my father would have called a "holy roller," and the color, pageantry, and ritual of the pre-Vatican II Roman Catholic Church. Tied to no denomination, it was a conglomeration of both spectrums of Christianity, with a sprinkling of Jewish traditions as well for good measure. With a vowed life extended to all men and women regardless of marital status, and a priesthood that offered the Eucharist to everyone, including those who were divorced, the CRC afforded inclusivity, not exclusivity. What began as a prayer meeting held in a tiny living room in a row house in the Steel Valley part of Pittsburgh became an organization that had churches across the United States, each a spoke of the wheel from the hub that was the Mother House in the Bishop's living room.

When I first clapped eyes on the Bishop, he was a short, stout man, with slicked-back silver-gray hair, penetrating gray-blue eyes, and a booming voice. He was dressed in a cassock, essentially a big zipped-up bathrobe. I remember his hands, small, delicate, not quite belonging to the rest of his body. Treated like a hothouse flower, he never climbed a set of steps without someone walking behind and before him to offer assistance. Always a small table appeared seemingly from nowhere whenever he sat down, complete with a glass of water, tissues, his reading glasses, and bible. No one who had a contagious illness was allowed near him, and his meals were prepared especially for him. He was the one and only Bishop, the shepherd of souls, under the one true Shepherd, Jesus.

By turns, the Bishop could be charming, angry, gentle, threatening, and manipulative, which I suppose is really just another version of charming. He had the final say on everything that happened in the CRC, and everyone consulted with him in every matter, from the order of the services to what food they would serve at events. The common joke was that "the Bishop said ..." was the eleventh commandment. The reactions of his congregation to his autocratic rule varied from fear and awe to complaints and vitriol, and the Bishop's reaction to his congregation was general distrust and displeasure most of the time. He even told the story of going to god and saying that he would disband the Chapter and the Priesthood and shut the whole damn thing down. He had railed to god that no one was obedient. God's response promptly told the Bishop that the Chapter were his brides, not the Bishop's, the priests were god's priests, not the Bishop's, and that the Bishop could do nothing about it.

The Church began as a prayer meeting that met once a week in the Bishop's living room and, over the years, had expanded to churches across the country and even a school in Africa. The Bishop's preaching style was that of an evangelist storyteller, who by turns could enchant, elicit laughter or tears, or come down on those with whom he was angry like a ton of bricks. While he demanded and pushed for sacrifice from everyone, what he frequently pointed out was true; there were no locks on the doors, and nothing and no one would ever stop anyone from leaving if they chose to do so. The Bishop also had an innate sense of how to touch the guilty conscience in people so that individuals gave sacrifices with seemingly willing hearts, even if that willingness came at the expense of personal integrity.

In the time I spent within the confines of the CRC, for all its protestations of inclusivity, there were divisions. There were Chapter members—and there was everyone else. There was the Priesthood—and there was everyone not in the Priesthood. And above it all sat the Bishop—the founder, the man with the plan, the one chosen by god to make it all happen. The proof of his stature as the prophet was his stigmata. During the Lenten season, the Bishop would bleed from wounds in his hands and from his side. Like the founder of the Franciscans, St. Francis, the Bishop shared in the passion of Christ.

I would have little interaction with the Bishop on a personal level over the coming years. The priests and other male deaconates constantly surrounded him. Few women were included in this inner circle. My one and only interview with him occurred when St. Xavier's Chapel imploded on itself. I found in that meeting a man saddened by the inconstancy of those he trusted and bewildered over how to manage the damage that others perpetrated on those who had faithfully served there.

The holiness of the CRC was held up as a standard for other congregations to emulate; we were constantly told that god made us the head and not the tail. But it was clear from my time in the CRC that the human beings in positions of authority had feet of clay and made mistakes, sometimes horrendous ones. Tales of sexual assault coming from the church established in New Jersey almost closed it down. When Fr. Thomas's wife left him, his relationship with one of his flock would lead to St. Xavier's Chapel closing as well. When the harm was done by those whom we were taught to revere and believe were conduits for god, it made their crimes that much more heinous.

In the beginning, when I was a "lamb," a newly born Christian, I had no knowledge of any of these past or future events. I went to the prayer meeting week after week, seeing it as a place of refuge from the ordinariness of my everyday life. I pitched in to help clean up after the services and learned all of the songs we sang by heart. It was a time of settling in, of feeling accepted and acknowledged. But change is inevitable, and it was coming in ways I couldn't begin to imagine.

Sharon Downey

Mr. Fox

I had never heard of the folktale "The Ruby Red Fox" until listening to recordings entitled "The Dangerous Old Woman" by Clarissa Pinkola Estes, the famed Jungian analyst and storyteller. In Dr. Estes' version of the tale, Mr. Fox lulls his victim bride to sleep with his soft, feathery tail, and she must fight to stay awake and overcome his seduction with her knowledge of the truth. An old woman who comes to the engagement party and produces the bloody hand of a bride murdered by Mr. Fox rescues the potential bride. In Dr. Estes' exposition on the story, she spoke of how each of us has met a Mr. Fox, whether he takes the guise of a person, an idea, or an addiction. Mr. Fox lures us to sleep by the flicking of his white tail and reassures us that we are misguided in our distrust of him. Dr. Estes described the old woman as the part of the psyche that is the protector, who watches over us, who shouts out to us, warning us not to fall asleep under the charms of Mr. Fox, but to wake up and realize that this somnolence is another form of death, the death of our souls.

When I met Fr. Thomas, I had my own inner old wise woman shouting at me, warning me to run and not turn back. I didn't listen to her, of course. As pastor of St. Xavier's Chapel, Fr. Thomas was a member of the Priesthood, under the Bishop, who was the head of the CRC. My friends who attended the church in the Mon Valley obeyed him and followed his guidance. Grace called him her shepherd, acknowledging him as her spiritual "covering." She was completely assured that he would never lead her astray. The idea of being obedient to someone else's direction on the basis that god would bless you for your obedience—even if you knew in your heart the path they were leading you on was wrong—had my inner old wise woman jumping up and down with fright. Unlike the Mr. Fox in the story, Fr. Thomas was certainly not a murderer. But his attempts to lure people to sleep, to become unconscious, to not question or disagree with him, to give over to him and the church all that he asked, was markedly like a seduction. Fr. Thomas would begin by wooing a potential victim, giving them extra attention, sharing "a word from the Lord," and even flattering them. After building up their trust, Thomas would launch his campaign to break his victims down. Teasing became belittling and then morphed often into harsh criticism. Thomas demanded more and more of people, expecting greater and greater sacrifices of time, money, and devotion.

My reaction was to feel a wall going up each time he attempted to lure me into a closer, more confiding relationship with him. Like with my relationship with god, even my relationship with my own father, I would not allow myself to cross certain boundaries. I recall hearing a wise woman saying once: "If you don't give me your power, you won't drink my Kool-Aid." I was not even going to touch the glass the Kool-Aid came in.

I gave Thomas the public respect his Priesthood in the CRC demanded; I stood up when he entered a room, I called him Father, I politely listened to what he had to say. When he pressed me to submit all facets of my life to him, even the private, I demurred. "You need to ask for permission for everything," he told me, "and not just in spiritual matters. Everything in life affects your spiritual life."

When finally, tired of being browbeaten, I made an effort to comply with this demand, it felt false, and we both knew it. I called him one night at home. My boss had offered me a new position at work. I asked Thomas if I should take it. He was abrupt. "You keep your benefits?" he asked.

"Yes," I answered, mystified by the question. I wasn't changing my employer, just my duties.

"OK, you can do it." He hung up with a mumbled, "God bless."

I hung up, feeling like a fool. I had obviously interrupted something, and he was annoyed with me.

I tried once more to obtain permission for something in my personal life. I wanted Tracy, another member of his congregation, to travel with me and my parents to Florida. When I asked Thomas about this, he said, "You know, people used to travel with their own priests so they had someone along to say mass and give spiritual counsel."

I sighed. "Yes, I'm sure they did. Can we go or not?"

"Yes, you two can go." He turned away from me. I had taken the fun out of the conversation, and he had lost interest.

***

In the weeks before his birthday each year, Thomas would make pronouncements like "A really loving church would get their pastor a _____ for his birthday, for all the suffering he has to do on account of them being such a bunch of sinners." If you blessed him, gave to him, did for him, god would bless, give, and do for you. That was his attitude. One year, after he moaned and complained that the other priests had nice new dress cassocks (essentially a long dress overcoat, with red trim and a sash belt) and that his was ratty and old, the congregation chipped in to purchase him a new one. I was by then the church's sacristan, charged with everything that had to do with the conduct of services; priestly garments, including cassocks, fell under that broad umbrella. I used a tape measure to take his neck, chest, waist, hip, and arm-length measurements. "Don't you need the inseam?" he asked.

"No." I put the tape measure at his right shoulder and told him to hold it there with his left hand. Then I stooped to see where the opposite end grazed the top of his shoe. "This is a dress, not a pair of pants." I was not going to put my hand between his legs. He scowled down at me.

I took the measurements to an old woman who made cassocks in a dusty shop on the South Side of the city. She frowned at the piece of paper with my scrawled numbers. "Can't be right," she croaked. "No one is built like this."

I twisted my lips and shook my head. "They're right."

"Does he eat?" she asked.

"Coffee and cigarettes."

She was right, of course. She was used to sewing for people who had some body fat, who had roundness of belly, who weren't all angles and hard, unyielding lines. Thomas was thin, and clothes hung on him like a runway model. He had no belly, no waist or hips. Dressed completely in black from head to toe, he looked even more angular and hard.

***

Repeatedly, Thomas cajoled, suggested, and even demanded that I become a resident at the Mother House church. I think he would have actually preferred if I moved into the basement at St. Xavier's Chapel. I refused repeatedly, telling him I already had a home. "God wants more from you," he would tell me. By then I felt I was giving god more than his fair share. I wanted peace and quiet and security. I wouldn't find any of those things living in the chaotic maelstrom of the Mother House. Another attempt at exercising control over me was laughable at best. During one summer bible school carnival finale, I was there to clean the chapel. The outside of the church was a whirling dervish of activity—kids screaming and running rampant, while the adults desperately tried to keep order. Thomas came into the church and spotted me polishing the brassware. "Why aren't you outside?"

I stared at him. "Because this is filthy." I held up a blackened censer.

"You should be in the children's ministry; you belong there," he said. His jaw was set hard, as it always was when he made one of his pronouncements.

I laughed derisively. One week he was telling me I belonged in the music ministry, then the cleaning ministry, and now this. "I hate brats," I said, rubbing the brass with polish. He glared at me and stomped back outside.

***

There were those in the Mother House who saw Thomas as abrasive, rude, and demanding. He would never have won any popularity contests. What the people in the Mother House didn't realize was that the cohort Thomas had collected around himself as his flock gave to him as good as he dished out to all of us. It came out in public at the dinner party for Grace and Annie's class, held after they had taken their professed vows. I was part of the kitchen crew, helping to serve food and clean up afterwards. It was a hot day and the kitchen was sweltering. Each of the new professed Brides of Christ gave a little speech after dinner. Grace got up, and in the course of her talk, called Thomas a "little Hitler." Now of course, no one really thought she meant Thomas was sending millions to the gas chambers, but the analogy wasn't a very flattering one. I'm fairly sure Grace simply meant Thomas could be like a martinet, demanding and capricious.

After the speeches were over, into the chaos of the kitchen, strode Thomas. I was struggling with wrapping leftovers in cling wrap and getting nowhere fast. One of the older professed women was working near me. She was the Counsel for the Chapter, acting as the go-between when vowed members and their superiors had issues. Thomas came over and stood next to me. "Tell her," Thomas whined, pointing to my companion. "Tell Sister So and So what a good pastor I am."

I glared at him. I was hot, tired, and in a losing battle with a box of cling wrap—and he wanted his ego stroked. I sighed. In a low tone, I curtly replied, "Jesus Christ is your defense, not me." I had hit him with a classic line from Chapter life. In culpa, where people had the opportunity to accuse others of faults against the holy rule, the aspirant director had taught us that if anyone falsely accused us of anything, we had no right to rebuttal; Christ was our defense, if he chose to be. I looked over at Sister So and So. She could barely keep herself from laughing. Thomas, on the other hand, looked as if I had just slapped him. At that point, I didn't have the energy to care what he thought. I had achieved my goal, which was to silence him. He left the room, albeit in a huff.

***

A few year later, after a service at St. Xavier's, Thomas demanded that Sr. Catherine, the head sacristan, and I take communion to Pat, an elderly member of the congregation. Pat was then in the hospital recovering from surgery. She was not in Chapter but had been among the first tithers at St. Xavier's and faithfully attended Mass and prayer meetings. Sr. Catherine was upset about taking the communion to Pat herself. The pyx, a small gold box container that held the host, was placed in a linen cloth and then into a linen-lined bag that was worn over the neck on a cord so that the bag lay over the deaconate's chest under the shirt. This was fine for a man, for whom unbuttoning a clergy shirt to remove the pyx would present no problem. Sr. Catherine, however, would have to open her blouse and expose her bra to get at the pyx.

Thomas wouldn't hear of Sr. Catherine's reservations. He told her she would manage. Evidently Sr. Catherine felt she couldn't or wouldn't tell Thomas no, and so off we went to the hospital. After entering Pat's room, Sr. Catherine turned her back to us to undress and produce the pyx. After receiving communion, Pat asked where Thomas was.

"Back at the church," I explained. I could see the hurt and puzzlement on her face. "Hasn't he come to see you?"

"No," Pat answered sadly, "and I've been here all week. Why hasn't he come?" I told her I didn't know, but I would ask him. We chatted about her health and the care she was receiving. I told Pat that I hoped she would soon make a full recovery, and then Sr. Catherine and I drove back to the church.

We found Thomas outside struggling with a battered charcoal grill, trying to straighten its frame. I posed Pat's query to him.

"Did you tell her I'm busy?" He banged on the rusted metal.

I smiled. "Jesus Christ is your defense, not me. I'm only relaying the message." I thought he was about to pick up one of the tools and hurl it at me. As I was leaving a few moments later, Thomas shouted at me.

"Aren't you going to stay and help?"

"No," I answered, "you'll manage just fine." I left, laughing to myself.

In some ways, Thomas reminded me of my own father, both of them alienating and self-absorbed. Thomas was much more open in his desires and demands than my father, asserting his "rights" and privileges in a calculating and cold way. Both triggered the same response from me, which was to wall myself off from them and proceed on my own way. Yet with Thomas, I was unable to resist bursting the pompous bubble he created for himself by bringing him back down to earth with an occasional verbal jab. He wanted obedient minions that followed orders. His congregation was full of those, like me, who contradicted him and spoke truth to power.

In the story of "The Ruby Red Fox," the old woman, who is the inner voice of consciousness, bids the young woman "Lest your life be taken, I bid you strong, to stay awake." I was an unconscious participant in my life before I came to the CRC, and for the first years of my life within the confines of the Church, I struggled between waking and sleeping. Fr. Thomas played a leading role in my somnolence and ironically helped in my struggle to awaken to my life.

Money and God

Everyone, I think, grows up with a money story. We worship money, struggle with money, and even try to ignore money. I lived in a household where money was the undercurrent in every discussion or action. How much would something cost, where would the money come from, what debts were owed? Needs versus wants. My parents struggled for every penny they earned and were not above telling my brother and me that money didn't grow on trees or fall from the sky.

In a religious context, Christ mentions money more times than any other topic in the New Testament, including sex, heaven, and hell. A favorite I heard quoted often was the last sentence of Matthew 6:24: "You cannot serve both god and money." It really isn't surprising. Money is nothing more than a measurement of value. What you treasure is what you think about, worry about, dream about. Everything has a price; everything seems to be for sale. And while I could understand the need for money to support the church, the efforts to fundraise in the CRC could be taken to extremes.

Tithing was a huge issue in the CRC. Everyone in Chapter was supposed to tithe ten percent of their gross income. Even the IRS allows deductions—but not god. We heard sermons that told us that if we trusted and gave accordingly, god would reward us. After I had been coming to the prayer meetings for a year, I started to tithe. I had a dream of Thomas speaking with Grace, asking her why I wouldn't give him a sweater I was holding. I heard the discussion in the dream, watching it take place, both of them behaving as if I wasn't present. It was an episode out of my everyday life, reflecting how my father had always interacted with me by asking my mother why I was doing something or behaving a certain way. He would not or could not interact with me directly; he always used my mother as an intermediary.

Now there was this dream where Thomas was behaving exactly like my father by not confronting me; instead he used Grace as a buffer. I didn't know then about Jungian dream analysis, how every character in your dreams represents an aspect of your own psyche. I cast these two outside individuals in my life as stand-ins for my mother and father and the mother/father parts of my own psyche.

My first mistake was to tell Grace the dream. "You need to tell Fr. Thomas," she said. "I'm sure that means something for you." The following Monday night, I sat down at his table in the basement during the break.

"You wanted to know why I wouldn't give you the sweater," I explained. He nodded his head, tapping one long finger on the tabletop.

"Tell me the entire dream one more time," he demanded. After I went through the sequence of events again, he said, "I'll need to talk to the Bishop about this. I think I know what it means, but I want to confer with him." The following Monday evening, Thomas called me over.

"The Bishop agrees with me; this dream is telling you to tithe. The sweater is what you value, and you need to give that to god."

"Oh." This was not the response from him I was expecting. I was certain the dream had some deep spiritual meaning. Turned out god was simply asking me to pony up.

"You will be stepping out in faith." Thomas continued, despite my troubled expression. I was still working at the bank, still making very little, and the prospect of contributing a tenth of my income daunted me. "God will test you on this. If doing his will was easy, there wouldn't be any merit in it." I nodded my head and rose from my seat. "The Bishop did say he never heard of anyone being called to tithe in a dream. He was impressed," Thomas added.

I suppose that was to encourage me. Did I logically say no to the demand? Of course not. I ignored the alarm bells going off in my head and I started to give ten percent of my income to St. Xavier's Chapel, even though some months it meant dipping into my thin savings to cover my other obligations. But if I persisted despite the hardships, then god would bless me financially, I had been taught. I just had to be patient and keep writing those checks.

Of course, after my mother saw me writing a check to the CRC and the amount of it, she was incensed. I paid her a monthly rent that was much higher than the amount of my tithe, but that didn't stop her from raising her voice and letting me know exactly what she thought. My parents dropped $10 in the collection plate at church every Sunday—and that was enough, in her opinion. Writing checks for more than $100 a month to an organization she considered pure evil was the last straw. "Don't ask me for anything, ever!" she railed. Not that I ever did. "If you can afford that stupidity, you can pay your own way for everything else!"

In retrospect, the dream I had about withholding a sweater from Thomas had undoubtedly more to do with my own inner reservations of my ongoing relationship with him and the church. I wonder now how much different my life would have been if I had had access to a wise counselor, trained in the decoding of dreams, to help me unearth the truths shown to me in that dream.

***

"Fundraiser" soon became a dirty word to me after I joined Chapter. It was always something—spaghetti dinners, bake sales, raffles, special collections. Money was at the front and center of every business meeting for the Chapter. Lent was especially bad; it was the season of denial and giving. The elders gave each ministry within the CRC a dollar amount they had to raise. Selling people raffle tickets was a con game. I'll buy yours if you buy mine. Finding the rare bird who was not in Chapter and who had no tickets to sell was like finding an albino peacock—and everyone wanted to pluck those feathers. There were dues for Chapter, fees for office books, and collections for other events throughout the year. I simply ignored all of the other calls for cash and only paid my tithe. That was hard enough some months.

In the Roman Catholic Church my parents attended, missionaries came asking for money and the retired religious asked for donations. Poor boxes collected spare change in the vestibule, and boxes stationed in the parking lot collected clothes and shoes. The church also held blood drives and food collections, and outside groups like the Lions and the Knights of Columbus collected money for their causes at the church doors. I never saw or heard of any other charity organization collecting or asking for donations from the CRC. The CRC made a practice of distributing gift bags to the poor on Valentine's Day, in honor of the Bishop's mother, and giving baskets of fruit and other goodies to the Passionist nuns. The gift bags held copies of a book about the Bishop's mother, which was simply another means to proselytize. The CRC seemed to not be in the business of charity work.

Grace had told me that ten percent of the collections, or a tithe of the tithes, helped the needy in India and supported a school there. But I saw the need in our own backyard: the unemployed, those struggling to raise children on one income, the elderly poor trying to make ends meet. We were a self-contained bubble of prosperity in the midst of a ghetto, and the Bishop liked nothing better than to remind us all of that fact. We were worker bees, expected to go out and bring back the nectar to the hive. Women at some of the out-of-town churches worked cleaning jobs at the homes of the wealthy and turned over all of the proceeds to their home churches so that their pastor and his wife did not have to work. Others worked long hours making candy and baked goods for sale.

Thomas's wife, Lena, worked as a nurse so that Thomas didn't have to have a paying job. He was available to the Bishop, going out for long lunches and drives, sitting and smoking on the back patio, and working around the CRC. In the months before Lena left Thomas, he questioned me one morning as to whether or not I was tithing. By this point I had no qualms about answering such a stupid question with a sharp-tongued answer. "What? Is the writing on my checks too small for you to read? Maybe you need new glasses," I told him.

"Just checking to see if you are doing what you promised," he mumbled.

Grace later told me that Lena was endorsing the checks and cashing them. The money never made its way into the church's account. Lena then left Thomas, spending the money on herself.

Was it the first time that something like this had happened within the CRC? I don't know. But I had my doubts. To my shame, I kept writing those checks until the day I left the Chapter. Was I worried that god would not bless me? I had managed to stay employed all of those years, moving from job to job with increases in pay, always paying my bills and saving money. But I was able to do the same when I stopped tithing. I came to understand that a gift given out of fear, rather than from the desire to serve and contribute, diminishes both the gift and the giver.

Sharon Downey

Miracle Service

Growing up Catholic, I was familiar with stories of miracles. People went to places like Lourdes, where they drank and bathed in the water and claimed to be cured of all sorts of ailments. Or some holy person died and people prayed to them for healing. And the "miracle," if it held up under scrutiny, helped to make that holy person a saint. Not to mention all of those miracles Jesus did back in the day, restoring eyesight with mud made from spit and dirt, making lunch for 5,000, and forcing old Lazarus to come back from the big sleep. But all of these instances were rare and unusual and happened either long ago or in special places. No one, it seemed, put much stock in ordinary, everyday miracles like getting your period when you were convinced you were pregnant, or when mean Mr. Smith, your tenth-grade math teacher, came down with bronchitis and the big exam you hadn't studied for was canceled.

The CRC, on the other hand, lived by the idea that miracles were a natural extension of preaching the gospel, that telling others about the gift of salvation would unleash a flood of miracle-working power, as it had done for Christ and the apostles. Before big weekend Chapter events, the CRC usually held miracle services. The idea for these stemmed from the services Kathryn Kuhlman conducted. She was the evangelist in the Pittsburgh area who had proclaimed the Bishop's "Paul" experience; like Saul of Taurus, who was knocked off his donkey, and blinded, the Bishop had had a direct encounter with Christ. During her miracle services, Ms. Kuhlman would call out healings that the Holy Spirit was performing and people would come up for prayer with her and be "slain in the spirit." They'd fall to the ground as she touched them.

The Bishop followed Ms. Kuhlman's "protocol" for how a miracle service was set up. The choir would first sing praise songs, and often someone would get up and give testimony about a healing they had received at a prior miracle service. Then the Bishop would get up and preach on the word from scripture he had been given by the Lord, saying, "The Word went forth to heal them." The choir would start up again, always the same hymn—"How Great Thou Art"—and the Bishop would call out one or two healings. Those who had been touched came up to be prayed over. After the proclaimed healings received prayer from the Bishop, a line would form with everyone else who wanted prayer.

A group of the priests and deaconates flanked the Bishop. It was their task to "undergird" the Bishop with prayer while he was dealing with the crowd. The ushers would split the line in two at the head of it. They would take the next two people in line and place one directly in front of the Bishop, while the next person stood to the side. The Bishop would go from side to side, listening to each request. Some simply received a blessing, some a stern lecture. Others the Bishop prayed over for what seemed like minutes. The ushers were there to catch those slain in the spirit from hitting the floor and hurting themselves. A few people lost consciousness for several moments, while others only staggered back a few steps and then walked back to their seats unaided.

Monthly miracle services started happening at the YMCA in downtown Pittsburgh at lunchtime. Grace and I would walk there, along with whomever else she could charm into coming with us. On one occasion, it was my turn to head up the aisle. I had struggled with back problems for most of my life. I was diagnosed with sciatica, which would leave me with a burning sensation in my left leg and pain that ran all the way down to the bottom of my foot. The only things that would help were aspirin and a heating pad to loosen the tight muscles in my lower back.

That particular day, the Bishop called out a healing for a bad back. I looked around. That could be just about anyone, I thought. Loads of people have back trouble. Grace looked at me and poked me in the arm. "That's you. Get up!" she whispered. "Go get your blessing!" I still hung back and eventually got into the line that was forming down the middle of the hall.

When I got to the front of the line, I choked out the words, "My back."

The Bishop pointed at me. "You're the one the healing was called out for," he said, almost in a chiding way, like *What took you so long to get up here?* He motioned for one of the ushers to bring up a chair.

I must have conveyed my thought, *What are you doing?*

The Bishop just smiled. "Sit."

I plunked my butt down like an obedient dog. "Put both of your legs out in front of you."

I stretched my legs out.

"This one is shorter than this one. Now watch." The Bishop bent down and put his hand under the ankle of my left leg. It stretched to match the right in length. I felt a burning pain in my left hip. "Thank you, Jesus!" the Bishop crowed. "Only God can make a leg grow!" He let go of my ankle, and the ushers helped me stand. The Bishop prayed for a bit with his hand on my head, and then he turned away, praising god for healing me. I turned and walked back to my seat. Had I seen what I thought I saw happen? I put my hand on my left hip, sat down, and stared at my feet. They didn't look any different. Grace was gleeful, smiling at me. We stayed until we had to walk back to the office.

Can I say I received a healing that day? For that day, maybe. I've had back pain on and off over the years. I often experience it when I've over exerted myself or when I neglect to exercise to keep my muscles stretched and limber. I've had physical therapy for the pain and chiropractic treatments. I can't say that my legs are the same length. Many people have a functional leg-length discrepancy due to problems with the pelvis. I've discovered the benefits of yoga to keep my joints from becoming stiff, but it requires constant work. "Losing your healing" was a problem with the receiver, never the giver, in the eyes of the CRC; your own doubt and lack of faith would cause you to go back to the problem. God gave miracles freely, but it was entirely up to you to hold on to them.

All True Vows

Joining Chapter

When I first started working at the bank, across the street was a hole-in-the-wall hot dog shop called Wiener World. I went in almost every morning to buy coffee before going to work. I know what you're thinking—buying coffee from a hot dog shop is a bit weird, even dangerous; it would probably taste like the grease from the fryers. But the coffee was hot, not bad at all, and inexpensive. Behind the counter was the same collection of harried, tired workers, dodging around one another in their tiny workspace, struggling to keep the long line of customers moving. So many of the customers were regulars that when the servers saw us they would automatically grab the correct size Styrofoam cup—hey, it was the eighties, after all—and start filling it with the correct amounts of cream, sugar, and potent black java. How the hell they remembered people's orders was beyond me, but somehow they did. So the one morning when I shouted to the woman behind the counter that I wanted tea, not coffee—I had the beginnings of a sore throat and thought it would help—she dropped the cup of coffee she held in her hand in surprise. Her face showed dismay, puzzlement, and sheer disgust, all rolled into one. I had thrown a wrench into the fine-oiled machinery of a morning routine and had broken the spell.

Just as I was always supposed to drink a large with cream and sugar, it was a forgone conclusion among the group at St. Xavier's Chapel, that I would join Chapter. It was merely the progression of how things worked in the CRC. People came to a prayer meeting or mass. They started tithing and then maybe joined a ministry group, like the prayer ministry or one working with the children. After a year of this, they signed up for Chapter and became a vowed member. The CRC was nothing more than a vehicle for people to live a vowed life. For me to say no to the call of god would be akin to that request I had made for tea, not coffee—unthinkable.

***

The book for signing up for Chapter sat on the counter at St. Xavier's Chapel. You signed your name, stating your intent to become an aspirant and start the journey to becoming the Bride of Christ. I hesitated, letting weeks go by without signing my name. I had no idea what Chapter was like, what the requirements were. I had never set foot in the Mother House, where the CRC held the weekly Chapter meeting. I decided to ask Grace about it.

"What do you all do when you are in Chapter?" I asked.

She smiled her beatific smile. "Well, you have to read your office every day. We fast on Wednesdays until we eat dinner together. We give hours every week in service. And sometimes there are special services on Sundays." Her explanation was quick, calm, simple. No biggie. This Chapter thing would not take over your life, she seemed to be reassuring me.

"And the rewards! Oh, when you're in heaven, you will be that much closer to the Lord. He keeps his Brides very close." Somehow, she made heaven sound like a club, with some souls squeaking through the back door, and some, like the Brides of Christ, having VIP status.

"I know you were meant for this, Sharon," she went on. "I know that god is calling you to the vowed life. You just have to say yes."

I was still troubled. Her response wasn't so much an answer as it was a sales pitch. But she was my friend. She wouldn't want anything that was wrong for me—I hoped.

Moreover, yes, there were people who never took vows, who just came to the prayer meetings or Bible study, week after week. But you felt sorry for them, like they were stuck in the vestibule, unable to move up to the main part of the sanctuary with everyone else. There was an attitude of, *When are they going to get it together?* Or even worse: *Well, they missed the boat. Too bad for them.* Some in Chapter viewed them almost as second class. Just a subtle thing could make the difference. Each time a Chapter member received communion, a sacristan rang a bell, a single "ting," signifying the Lord and his Bride were together. No such bell rang for outsiders. They were they and we were we. We were all on the same train, heading to glory—but there were the first-class seats and then there was everyone else.

The offer of a vowed life was something that both was attractive and repelling to me. Sacrifice was something I had a life degree in, but my soul struggled against giving myself away. There I was, a twenty-six-year-old adult, who on the outside appeared to have her act together—a steady job, money in the bank, studying for my bachelor's degree at Pitt—but inside was still very much a scared and lonely child. By contrast, when I joined Chapter, my brother was twenty-four and in graduate school. We passed like two ships in the night; I worked full time and went to church, and he was either working at his part time job, going to class, or studying. Two years later, in 1989, he married his high school sweetheart. We didn't talk very much about my choice to take vows. Looking back, he seemed more mature than I was; he knew where he was going and had a path to get himself there. I was waiting for life to happen to me, while sticking to a safe, boring routine.

To me, saying no to joining the Chapter seemed ungrateful. God offered the opportunity to take vows as a gift, and of course, it was just rude to say no. Taking this step was a natural progression I had seen others take. Everyone in the Church simply expected others to step up and take that yoke upon their backs and choose the "closer walk with Jesus Christ." After all, who would not want to be among the insiders, those closest to the divine? Didn't I have a debt of gratitude to repay for all that Christ had done for me? Wasn't Chapter, in a deep spiritual and psychological sense, already so familiar to me? Ritual, sacrifice, silence—things my waking mind could not comprehend and yet were a part of my very core. The vow I had made to god as a frightened sixteen-year-old begging for my father's life never resurfaced in my mind as I struggled with the decision to join Chapter. It lay dormant in my subconscious, suppressed along with all of the other times I had acquiesced, giving up my desires and dreams.

I gave my choice to join Chapter very pretty beribboned reasons, of course, dressing it up to have it make sense to the linear, logical mind I'd inherited from my father. I was doing this for my family; my sacrifice would gain them favor with god and a place in heaven. I was simply obedient to the call of god to become his Bride. But there was no such call, no inner voice saying *Give this to me*. There was silent pressure, guilt (which I had dined on since childhood), and the expectations of those already in Chapter.

***

When I announced at home that I was joining Chapter, my parents' reaction was devastating. While I never expected them to be overjoyed with my choice, I was completely unprepared for the outpouring of grief and anger my decision unleashed. My father was the one in tears, sitting in the living room that afternoon, a towel pulled over his head, weeping, choking out little sobs. My father never cried. The last time I saw tears on his face was at my grandmother's funeral some sixteen years prior, but now he cried as if I were dead.

My mother reacted as I expected her to, with fury and bitterness. "Look at your poor father and what you are doing to him." Her face contorted in rage. "Is this what we struggled to raise you for, to have you run off and join a bunch of nut jobs? I suppose next you'll be telling me you'll be moving in there with them and you'll forget all about us." My attempts to explain, to smooth things over, to tell her I loved her and my father and never meant to hurt them, fell on deaf ears. "Go, get out." She waved me away from her. "Go be with those people, since you love them all so much." Her reproaches ripped my heart open.

In my bedroom, kneeling on the floor, I wept bitterly, rocking back and forth, crying until I was choking on the tears, with nothing and no one to comfort me. Going back downstairs to use the one and only phone in the house to call Grace or Annie was out of the question. All of those scriptures about family members set against one another as one chose Christ and the other didn't filled my head ("They will be divided…mother against daughter, daughter against mother… Luke 12:53) but left me only feeling more bereft. If Christ was there in that room with me that afternoon, he failed to make his presence known and left me to weep in my despair and anguish by myself. Countless others have written about their dark night of the soul—and I found myself in that deep pit of pain. I had nothing and no one on the outside of myself that could truly understand how I felt. I heard the voices of everyone within the CRC telling me that this was a merely a test. God wanted to see if I could keep faith with the vows I would take, if I would put Christ above my life, my family, everything I valued. What I didn't understand then was that the answer would never be outside of myself. I had to find that strength and courage from within—that was where the Divine lived. I had learned early in my life to view god as an external entity, transcendent, not immanent. Hours later, I finally crawled into bed and fell asleep, exhausted and empty.

    Had my father relived visions of his aunt, how she had left her family behind to become Sr. Inviolata? Did my mother picture herself alone with my father as he withdrew further into what I now believe was depression, her life even more hollow and empty? My search for autonomy was taking me to a place that expected me to give up all traces of it. Each of us was hurting, and none of us knew how to stop the pain. I could not go back on my word, I thought. I had signed the book; I had made a commitment. All of the classic truisms I had been handed my whole life rumbled around in my head. *You made your bed, now lie in it.* And, *Wish in one hand, shit in the other and see which piles up faster.* An icy truce fell over my house in the following days. No one spoke about my decision. We all ignored the elephant in the room.

***

    The following Wednesday, I sat with a group of strangers for my pre-aspirant interview with the elders. These were people the Bishop handpicked to lead and guide the church's ministry. Around a table sat Johnny, who had the look of a former bar bouncer; Grandma and Aunt Jo, the Bishop's mother and aunt; Victor, a prim man in a seersucker suit; and Billy, who simply stared at me during the entire process without speaking a word. I knew none of these people, and I was terrified. The only interviews I had ever had were job interviews, and those were scary enough. This was about my spiritual direction, and so the stakes, I was convinced, were much higher. I sat down in the lone empty seat, stiff, awkward, nervous, and completely convinced someone was going to ask me to leave at any moment. Self-confidence was something I had not yet acquired, even then. I was certain the group before me would hate me and that would be the end of my taking vows. I would fail before I had even begun. Shamefully, I was half hoping they would kick me out. Then I could avoid the whole thing altogether.

Victor was a balding, well-dressed gentleman, whose neat suit and tie looked out of place amidst the more casually dressed group. He began the meeting by saying that I spent all of my time at St. Xavier's Chapel and none at the Mother House. I sat there, my tongue glued to the roof of my mouth, unable to answer him. It was the truth, after all. This was my very first visit to the Mother House. I didn't know it then, but there was a great deal of animosity amongst the elders towards Fr. Thomas, especially from Victor. Those in authority viewed Thomas as a renegade, running his "own" church less than fifty miles from the Mother House. Thomas had evidently voiced the opinion that "his" people should meet for Chapter at St. Xavier's, much the way the out-of-town houses conducted their own Chapter nights. The fact that tithers at St. Xavier's Chapel, like myself, were not giving tithes directly to the Mother House also stirred ire in some of the elders. Johnny, a large man with a ruddy face, spoke up and pointed out that I tithed there faithfully. This apparent attempt to mollify Victor didn't work. Victor was also an old-line Baptist, who regarded much of what went on with the Chapter as popery. I would never understand why he was a part of this hybrid church of Catholic ritual and Protestant preaching, until I heard a saying attributed to the Mafia: "Keep your friends close and your enemies even closer."

Aunt Jo, the Bishop's mother's sister, focused her laser-blue eyes on me. She reminded me of the tough, no-nonsense teachers from my youth. She brought up my "skills" and noted I was good with numbers. On my application, I had put down that I worked at the bank and that I could crochet and sew. Although on the face of it, this was supposed to be a meeting to discern the applicant's spiritual readiness for vows, it had the undercurrents of a job interview and a financial review. What work could you do for the church and how much money did you have to donate?

Grandma, the Bishop's mother, a tiny, fragile looking woman, only piped up once, to ask me if I had a car. I said I had recently purchased one. "Good," she said quickly. "You'll need it to get here." Evidently, I passed the test, but Johnny, who was a jokester at heart, had to sneak in one bit of humor. He pointed to my application and said, "You did lie on here, you know."

I dropped my jaw and stared at him.

Chuckling, he said, "You can't possibly be this old." I plastered a smile on my face and assured him that the date was the truth.

I was worried about the whole interview for no reason. I later found out that the CRC never turned away anyone from taking vows, not even ex-cons, drug addicts, or alcoholics. Your past simply didn't matter. Often these very same people went on to take their professed vows, living clean lives and holding steady jobs. Those who were illiterate learned to read, and many were truly rehabilitated by the experience. Others lasted only a month or two, never to be heard from again, slipping back to the lives they lived before joining Chapter. I was amazed that the Church appeared to give no thought as to whether any of us truly had a religious calling. The door was open for anyone to try it.

The comment Johnny made about the lie regarding my age actually made sense. I was immature. At the age of twenty-six I was acting out a teenage identity crisis. I was a narcissist – and my martyrdom benefited no one but me. I was rebelling against the life my parents had told me was good for me by joining a group who would give me an entirely new set of rules to follow. I was exchanging one set of shackles for another. In a few short weeks, I would start my journey to become the Bride of Christ, with absolutely no idea what that truly meant or how it would change my life.

Sharon Downey

My Aspirant Step

My mother had been married and divorced before she met my father. It had been, in her words, a disaster. The marriage was nasty, brutal, and short. "I knew I was making a mistake as I walked down the aisle," my mother confided in me.

"Then why did you do it? Why not just back out?" I asked.

"I couldn't do that." She shook her head. "I would have embarrassed myself, him, our families." She paused in slicing potatoes for our dinner. "My mother knew it wouldn't work. And she was so disappointed when I left him. Divorce was a sin in her book. But she knew I wasn't happy. And then she always loved your Dad; he was perfect in her eyes." My mother looked at me, rolling her eyes at her mother's infatuation with my father. "That's because he was nothing like my first."

I wondered about that inward knowing—the small, quiet voice inside (or perhaps, having long been ignored, the stark-raving lunatic lunging at us) that tells us when we are about to make a mistake, a mistake that is more than just taking the wrong exit off a freeway or choosing the chocolate donut over the kale smoothie for breakfast. The kind of mistake that turns your world upside down, makes mincemeat of your equilibrium, and kicks your backside for good measure.

On a warm Sunday morning in June of 1987, I made such an error. It was Investiture weekend, three days of services, where those in the novitiate of the Chapter made their steps, moving closer to the day of Profession and Brideship. It was the day I would take my aspirant vows, the first step in that initial five-year struggle. I got up early and dressed in my requisite white outfit that I had purchased—a cotton ruffled eyelet skirt with a matching sleeveless vest and a long-sleeved jacket. I looked like a throwback to the sixties. All I needed was a circlet of flowers in my hair and a guitar strapped to my back. I trooped downstairs to find my mother drinking coffee in the kitchen. My father was still asleep. My mother's eyes flicked over me, up and down, checking out my outfit, taking note of my pale face, my dark circles under my puffy eyes from lack of sleep and crying. It was her fifty-ninth birthday. I had made the effort to purchase her a birthday cake and gifts, and we had celebrated the day before, but it had done little to stem her anger. "Today is not my birthday," she had announced, "tomorrow is the day, and my only daughter will not be here to celebrate it with me." How could the date chosen for the aspirant step, planned out a year in advance, be any worse?

"You're going through with it then?" She dropped the coffee cup into its saucer with a bit more force than necessary.

I mutely nodded my head.

Her eyes fixed on mine—that laser glare that always knew when I had misbehaved and attempted to cover it up, that knew when I was lying, the ultimate bullshit detector. "Well, you've made your bed. You best remember you're the one that has to lay in it." My mother turned her attention back to the Sunday newspaper and the crossword puzzle. She had written me off.

***

I drove to the Mother House through a glaze of tears. I kept telling myself this was part of my sacrifice, that god was asking me to turn my back on everything, and that no spiritual quest was without pain and suffering. It never occurred to me to just turn the car around and not go through with it. Some part of me deep down knew that to do that was no victory for me either, that I would just be complying with another set of demands. Either way, I was trapped.

My mother had walked down an aisle to marry someone she knew she didn't love, who was a danger to her, who was going to cause her untold suffering. I was making a vow to a god I could not see, uncertain if this was the right thing to do, or even if this sacrifice was being asked of me. I was repeating a pattern, one I could not see then. Our circumstances trapped my mother and me, and we were unable to say no.

I entered the living room of the Bishop's house. A portable altar was at the front of the room, set for mass, and my fellow new aspirants sat on benches that ringed the room. The day was hot, and sweat trickled down my neck. Our aspirant director, Sr. Mary Bernard, instructed us to remain in silence. I stole glances at the others on the benches, none of whom I knew. Young, old, fat, thin, male, and female—a type or look didn't predominate among us. Then the bell rang, and the Bishop along with two of the priests, including Thomas, entered. Mass began. The Bishop reminded all of us in his sermon of the great sacrifice of Christ and how the vows we were about to take were miniscule compared to the Lord's suffering.

When the mass was finished, Sr. Mary Bernard reminded us to remain in silence and instructed us to eat our lunch outside on the patio. Some of the older Chapter members looked over at us and smiled. I imagined they were thinking back to the days when they had been in our shoes. I picked at my food, unable to eat, my stomach churning. A short set of stairs led from the backyard patio to the parking lot behind. Just a quick dash up those steps and I could escape. But then where would I go?

After lunch, we gathered in the living room again. Sr. Felicity, the assistant mother superior, and a group of the class superiors were waiting to present us with our garb. One by one, we each came up to the kneeler. We were given our Ecce Homo (Behold the Man) medal of the suffering Christ on its long chain. Next, we received the single-volume office book that repeated the church liturgical calendar. Our daily reading of it would add our voices to the thousands around the world who read these same psalms and prayers, recalling the words of the apostle Paul to pray without ceasing. Next came the happy death cross, the silver corpus on a black wooden cross, which Sr. Felicity offered each of us to kiss. We were then given a copy of the "Holy Rule," a slim little pamphlet that we would be required to read daily for the next six months. It contained the guiding principles and rules of conduct for those in Chapter. On silver trays, the sacristans placed the perfectly starched caps and veils; each had a single cross stitched in red thread. Sr. Felicity presented them to our lips for us to kiss. Then one of the superiors placed the coverings on our heads. A sacristan handed each of us a small candle lit from the Paschal candle. She told us to extinguish it ourselves, for the moment.

We lined up in our order and processed out of the living room, down the patio, and through the sliding glass door. Two rows of chairs were on either side of the rooms leading to the altar. A statue of St. Clare, the patroness of our order, dressed in her brown robes and holding a monstrance, stood watching us from her niche next to the statue of St. Francis. The Bishop sat in front of the altar, flanked by two of the priests. There was a kneeler before them, where two of the elders stood dressed in white robes. Two deaconates pulled closed the wooden panel doors, sealing off the end of the hallway where the Bishop sat. Our candles were lit once again from the Paschal candle as we entered the doorway. Then we walked down the aisle, one by one.

The distance I walked to the kneeler seemed to defy the time-space continuum, taking infinitely longer in my mind then it did in reality. I heard a strange buzzing in my ears, and while I knew people surrounded me, it seemed to me that I was alone, completely alone. Despite the lack of air conditioning, I shivered. I lowered myself onto the kneeler. To form a doorway around me, the elders held up a prayer shawl, a large rectangular piece of white polyester cloth trimmed with gold fringe. I was on a threshold, a liminal space, betwixt and between, where god would set me apart. Another of the elders held up in front of me a card that had the aspirant vows written on it. With the hand that held my candle shaking, I read the words quickly, in a hushed monotone voice, afraid to stop, afraid of stumbling over the words. I can still remember the one line: "I make this vow of my own free will." I suppose that was true, to a point. No one was holding a gun to my head. But if I had been asked right at that moment, *Why are you doing this?* I know now I would not have been able to answer. Ahead of me were lessons I needed to learn, experiences I needed to live through— ones I could not have imagined while kneeling on that kneeler.

I extinguished my candle, and someone helped me to stand in front of the closed panel doors that held brass knockers. Sr. Mary Bernard stood in front of one of the doors, smiling. She lifted her hand, held the knocker, and clicked on the door three times. From behind the door came the voice of the Bishop, "What do you seek from the Church of the Resurrected Christ?"

Sr. Mary Bernard replied in a loud voice, "Eternal life and a closer walk with Jesus Christ."

"Then enter his gates with praise and thanksgiving," the Bishop replied to her.

Sr. Mary Bernard knocked for each one of us. We were not worthy to knock on the door, the door that represented the heart of god. We hadn't been tested or tried yet, we were told.

I didn't agree with that idea at all. No one could know what it had taken for some of us to walk down that aisle.

The deaconates pulled the doors open from within. On the floor in front of the Bishop was a small pillow. Around his shoulders, he wore a prayer shawl lined in linen. In his hands, he held a pyx containing the consecrated host. I knelt before him, lowered my head, kissed the glass top of the pyx, and heard the Bishop speak to me. "You have truly left both father and mother, and I am pleased with your sacrifice."

Those close to him who heard this broke out into praises of "Jesus!" and "Glory to you, Lord!" I broke down in tears, and two of the deaconates helped me outside.

I suppose at that moment I should have felt vindicated, that my sacrifice of my family and my peace of mind was acceptable to god, that what my family felt was irrelevant, and what I wanted was inconsequential. In my mother's words, I had made my bed—and I found it to be a cold and lonely place. If I was expecting to find comfort there from god, there was none to be had. God was elsewhere—my sacrifice notwithstanding. Looking back, I realize how easy it would have been for someone, like Thomas, to mention my home life to the Bishop. This triumphant affirmation of my sacrifice bubbling up from his lips at that exact moment was both an attempt to soothe me, and at the same time, allow the belief that he was a conduit for god to continue.

After the service, all of the new aspirants were loaded into cars and driven to a celebratory dinner. I truly didn't realize at the time how much hard work and effort went into this whole weekend, how many hours of service everyone in the church devoted to keep this whole event running smoothly. Everything, from the decorations to the freshly pressed caps and veils to the food for countless meals, had to be prepared by someone. Tradition, I was to learn, was an obsession, and the carrying out of the orders of the Bishop an overarching commandment.

    I went home that evening, careful to put all of the items of my new garb into a bag so that I looked no different than I had when I'd left that morning. But the tension in my house was like a vibration, an underlying hum, live wires that might lead to an explosion when I least imagined it. I had embarked on a fifteen-year journey in this vowed life, one that would test my commitment to those vows, over and over again.

Truth in Advertising

As a young girl, I spent many hours waiting for my mother in the beauty parlor. My mother had latched onto a beautician named Camille. Camille drifted from salon to salon, taking her "heads" with her—or, at least my mother's. Having her hair permed and colored was the one treat my mother allowed herself, and the process seemed to take forever. To pass the time, I sat in an unoccupied dryer chair or a rickety stool in some dusty corner of whatever shop Camille was working in and read magazines. *Redbook, Ladies Home Journal, Family Circle*—they all had beautiful ads showing wonderful things my family didn't have, modeled by people who looked nothing like us. For those hours, my very active imagination let me live another life.

To advertise the Chapter, the CRC had printed up brochures. We were in the pre-internet days, so a paper pamphlet was the way to go. If you think it's odd to advertise for future nuns, brothers, or priests, just go online and Google "Franciscans" or "Benedictines" or any other order you like. You'll find webpages by the score, some with great photos and "meet the nuns" pages with personal stories of their callings. The CRC brochure was actually quite slick for its time. It featured a photo of beautiful young woman dressed in her garb kneeling before the altar, light pouring down on her from the adjacent window—a picture of holiness, purity, and serenity. Another photo showed a group of young people sitting in a circle outdoors, representing the different stages of the novitiate in their various types of garb, as a professed man played a guitar and led them in song. You could almost hear the strains of "Kumbaya." The brochures were on the counter of the first-floor break room at St. Xavier's Chapel and on a table near the tithe box at the Mother House. Like those glamorous ads I remembered from visiting the beauty parlor, someone had carefully designed these brochures to show a world and a way of life that was a fantasy. As in many cases, the advertising does not accurately portray the truth of the product. You are not the happy woman in the laundry soap ad, admiring the amazing fresh-smelling clothes in an immaculate laundry room. No, you are surrounded by piles of stinky underwear, your husband's filthy work clothes, and the bedding your sick child vomited on last night, as you stand in a dank basement with cobwebs in the corners. Reality, in other words, bites.

I found myself in the midst of my own reality crisis my first Wednesday night, my first Chapter meeting, after my aspirant step. It settled over me, like the oppressive heat of the back of the hall, where my class sat, the least and lowliest. It turned out that, like any other big organization, in the Chapter you had the worker bees and the slackers. A large part of every Wednesday evening was devoted to cleaning or setting up for some weekend event or to making food, canning, and the like. Work was never ending.

Our superior, Sr. Mary Bernard, squeezed in a small amount of time to teach us how to read the office book and to drill us in the basic rules, such as letting older members go before us and standing for anyone in authority when they entered a room. I just took the safest route and tried to stay on my feet as much as possible.

Every task was designed to be performed in the most difficult manner possible and to take the most amount of time to complete. I watched grown men and women washing Styrofoam dishes and cups instead of disposing of them. People were selected to serve the food for dinner in a tiny kitchen, but there was scarcely enough room for the people passing through with their empty plates, let alone room for someone to stand and ladle soup. One Wednesday night, I was assigned to clean the floor in one of the kitchens. "Where is the mop kept?" I innocently asked the superior who gave me the task. She looked at me as if I had grown a second head.

"Mop? No, no, you'll need to just get a bucket, some Simple Green (a cleaning product that smelled like death) and some rags." She told me I could find all of the above in the cabinet under the kitchen sink.

I tried to keep my mouth from dangling somewhere near my knees. I spent the next forty-five minutes on all fours, scrubbing that floor.

We frequently skipped the chanting of the Divine Office, which never made sense to me, despite the "Holy Rule" dictating that it was to be a part of the Wednesday night experience. As we were a contemplative order, the Chapter was to read this liturgy of the life of Christ every day. This meant having to read it hurriedly before bed once I finally got home. The business meeting was another excruciating process: a long list of upcoming events, volunteers that were needed for various duties, fundraisers such as hoagie sales and spaghetti dinners, and a list of services that would require being excused in order not to attend. We received Holy Communion as usually the last exercise of the night, and then we each had to ask the superior in charge of cleanup for permission to be excused to leave. I was often arriving home after ten and still had to read my office book and get organized for work the next day. I envied those who were going to get to sleep in. The alarm shattering my dreams at six, a mere six hours after I laid down, added to my misery. The pretty picture of kneeling in beautiful adoration and sublime silence was a myth.

The aspirant year was one of obedience—the first of the three vows of obedience, poverty, and chastity to be learned. The cross on our veils and caps at the back of our heads dangled over our spines to remind us that obedience was our backbone. What I slowly learned was that obedience without question was designed to rob you of your backbone, your will to stand up for yourself and say enough. I had always been an obedient daughter to my parents, even though I chafed against their ideas of what was "correct" behavior. But I knew deep down that they dictated their rules—although confining—out of love and fear, to keep me from harm.

I soon realized that my chief problem with Chapter would be my mind, the facile and quick-thinking gift I had been born with, which was neither desired nor appreciated in a religious. I had to learn to turn it off, or at least tame it. The link it had to my mouth was another issue. As I grew older, my ability to stifle whatever I thought from immediately thereafter tumbling from my lips, grew weaker. Biting my tongue, keeping quiet, going along to get along, would gain me nothing and eventually, I believe, lead to the biggest health scare of my life.

All True Vows

The Letter in My Office Book

When I was in eleventh grade, I signed up for Algebra II. If you had asked me why, I probably would have babbled something about college requirements and filling in an elective. Really, I don't know why I did it; I had no real interest in math—beyond figuring out how much money was in my wallet (and that was easy, as the amount was usually zero). I was spending hours in the evenings trying to do the homework by myself because the idea of asking for help would have seemed like cheating. My parents raised me to believe that if I couldn't handle this myself, I was just incapable of learning advanced algebra. I had made a huge mistake—which was particularly glaring after I received a D on my report card for the first nine weeks. Dropping the class was the most load-lightening event of that year.

Joining Chapter was also a mistake. My intended, the big JC, if he had assumed a corporeal presence, would have leaned up against a wall, his arms folded across his chest, shaking his head. *Didn't ask you to do this*, I could hear him saying. *Not your circus, not your monkeys.* But unlike my decision to drop algebra, I was stuck in paralysis about sticking it out in Chapter or leaving. It didn't help that knowing the reaction of my parents, particularly my mother, would be, *I told you not to do it.*

I kept a fantasy in my office book for my entire aspirant year. It was my letter of resignation. Not that it was required. People who wanted to quit just stopped showing up for Chapter. And while some of the superiors pursued their lost sheep, most were just allowed to drop off the lists without another thought. But I was always one to do the necessary paperwork. I wrote a simple letter stating I had made a mistake and was sorry to have put everyone through the bother. I would need to put it into the mailbox for the Chapter and then remove my veil and place it on the altar. The Chapter would then release me from my vows. No fuss, no muss. After all, the novitiate was the time for testing and trying out the vowed life. There was no shame in saying it wasn't right for me. Some people even delayed taking their professed vows, staying in the novitiate until they could be sure the ten-year commitment in the professed life was right for them.

I wrote the letter and put in my office book. I would take it out on Wednesday nights and read it, so often in fact that the paper was permanently creased, shiny from the oils in my fingers, the ink becoming smudged and feathered. Every time I read it, I would fold it back up and place it into the space between the book and its protective cover. I would look across the aisle at Sr. Mary Bernard, the aspirant director, her belly growing with her latest child. She wore the brown jumper that served as pregnancy garb and gently stroked her broadening girth. Guilt would well up in me, a familiar entity in my life. Raised a Catholic, and worse yet, a half Irish, half Slovak Catholic, guilt was a part of my daily diet, along with regret and remorse. My religious education taught me early on that you didn't blame god if your life sucked. Instead, it must be because you had done something to piss god off, and he was punishing you. If something good happened, you had to thank god. If you didn't, the good would disappear and god would replace it with bad. Every time Sr. Mary Bernard would teach us anything, she would stress that faith was our only hope. If we believed that god would be there for us, he would be, even when things were tough. If we were in Chapter, she reasoned we belonged there. Telling her I was leaving just seemed cruel.

One Wednesday night when I had been in Chapter a few months, the Counsel for the Chapter got up at the front of the hall and stated that two professed individuals had divorced the Lord and left the Chapter. We were all instructed not to speak their names again or to have anything to do with them in the future. Their Paschal candles that they had carried at their profession had been broken in two, and Chapter members had said the "Office of the Dead" for them.

I sat wide eyed, confused, and frankly, concerned. I didn't know those who had left (they were a married couple) and would not learn until much later their reason for leaving. The wife was ill, and she desired for her husband and herself to spend their life together without the burden of the religious life. All I knew at that moment was that these two people were to be shunned, treated as lepers, and that in the eyes of god they were dead. Divorcing the Lord, I would come to learn, meant that you were placing yourself in a particularly bad section of purgatory upon your death, where god would guarantee you would do some serious ass burning. You wouldn't merit hell, because you couldn't lose your salvation, but god would be totally pissed with you and might just leave you there until forever was almost up.

Of course, leaving while still in the novitiate was an entirely different matter than leaving once professed, but I felt certain that you would pay a price for turning your back on the god of the universe no matter at what point in the journey you did it. Factor in the thought that I believed I was between a rock and hard place with choosing to stay or leave, and I was basically screwed. So I kept reading and re-reading my letter of farewell and kept returning it to my office book. I never did turn it in.

A year later, at the celebratory dinner after my class had made our next step and become postulants, I approached Sr. Mary Bernard, now back from her maternity leave. "I'm still in Chapter because of you," I said, as if I were looking for someone to blame for my own lack of will. Fortunately, she took it as a compliment and then immediately deferred it to god.

"You are here because this is where you are supposed to be," Mary Bernard said, "and because this is where god wants you." She beamed at me, her warm brown eyes showering me with love. We embraced, and I felt like crying, which I knew she would have interpreted as tears of happiness. I had dug the hole I was in just a bit deeper. It was a mercy I didn't know at that moment how much deeper the hole I was digging for myself was about to become.

Sharon Downey

Sacristan Training: Cinderella Scrubbing Bottles

I was a young child when I watched on television the Rogers and Hammerstein version of *Cinderella*. I was completely enchanted. The story I knew so well came to life before me, with the gorgeous costumes, the sweet singing of Leslie Ann Warren, and the fairy godmother who makes magic. I watched a beautiful and kindhearted girl become a princess. The handsome prince walks in and makes her dreams come true, the reward for all of the long suffering she has endured. She is rescued by her prince—no more sitting by the fire for her.

Then you grow up and you realize that fairy tales are most definitely not reality. If you are waiting for a prince to rescue you, you're in for a hell of long wait. Poor old Cinderella was sitting in that dirt because she had no choice.

Now, I was Cinderella. Only there was no hearth, no little chair by the fire, and no smudges of dirt on my face. Instead, I had signed up to be a part of the sacristan training program, where Chapter members, primarily women, a few brave men, were trained to become part of the Priesthood as first deaconates, to care for the altars and chapels, and prepare for all of the services throughout the liturgical year. Chapter members signed up for the program and met every six weeks or so at the Mother House for teachings and practical learning. When ordained, I would handle such items as a tabernacle and a chalice. For now, I dusted, swept, washed windows, polished brass, ironed linens and vestments, and scurried about, lifting, carrying, cleaning—in general, acting much like Cinderella before the ball.

I was in my first postulant year, my second year in Chapter, on Holy Thursday evening before Easter. As part of my sacristan training, I bent over a laundry tub in a dank and dimly lit basement, up to my elbows in hot water. Old prescription bottles normally used to hold cough syrup had been repurposed to distribute various sacramental oils, like healing, anointing, and deliverance oils. Chapter members returned the bottles leftover from the previous year so that the sacristans could clean and reuse them. I know now that a strong dish detergent like Dawn would have cut the grease, but Peter, the sacristan trainer, had given me a bottle of cheap, generic pink dish soap. I took up my stand in this battle against grease right after dinner, with pans of hot water for soaking, pans of soapy water for washing, and more pans of hot water for rinsing. Some of the bottles still had the tiny descriptive labels on them, which I had to remove, picking them off with my fingernails. Above me, on the first floor, I could hear the sounds of the Holy Thursday readings of the passion and the singing of the choir. People came and went to the antechapel, where the only Eucharistic presence was kept until Saturday, to perform their "watch" time with the Lord. I saw them pass through the front door and head up the stairs. No one noticed Cinderella at her sink.

I had joined the sacristan program because... *Dear mother of all that is holy, why the hell did I join?* Because I needed to show that I was useful in order to be loved? Because this was a role where there was order in the midst of the usual chaos that was the CRC? Because Thomas wanted a sacristan from his own flock to care for "his" church, not someone "loaned" to him from the Mother House? The truth? Because I knew I was a fraud—that I would never be a true Bride of Christ. I made the decision to remain in Chapter not from love but from guilt—and if I'm honest with myself, more than a bit of masochistic pride. I was going to stick this out, no matter how much it hurt—because to admit I was wrong was too difficult for a thin-skinned idiot like me. In this empty relationship (at least on my side of the equation) I could put myself as close to the god I was marrying as possible, tend to his needs at the heart of this church, become a guardian of the tabernacle and the Eucharist, and so convince myself that I could stick this out, that I was needed. I would keep god's altar clean, his lamps lit. I would be the servant of the servants of god and make up for the blackness that I held within me.

So I scrubbed the bottles with brushes. I wasn't wearing a watch, and the basement didn't have a clock; I had no real idea of the passage of time. My back ached, and the hot water and cheap soap stung my hands raw. I felt sorry for myself and fought back tears. I finally heard footsteps coming toward me. It was Peter, my teacher. He looked at me and the mess around me, his jaw dropping open. "Are you still here?" he asked, his voice shocked.

I nodded glumly. "They won't come clean."

"That's enough for tonight, it's late."

"What time is it?" I asked.

"Twelve-thirty. Go home." He smiled at me weakly.

I looked around at the bins of bottles, dozens and dozens of them, clean ones placed on a towel atop the washing machine, others soaking in a bucket on the floor, bobbing in the hot water. I rubbed my hands on a sopping towel, my fingertips puffed and swollen. I had been in that basement for more than six hours.

"I forgot you were down here." Peter picked up the bucket and angled it into the sink. We used the damp towels to mop up the floor. "Leave everything in the sink to soak," he told me. "I'll get someone else to finish this tomorrow."

I looked into his dark eyes and saw pity and embarrassment in them. My eyes burned with unshed tears.

"It will get better," he told me gently.

I shrugged my shoulders, wished him goodnight, and climbed up the two flights to the antechapel to say goodbye to the Lord. Then I drove home to crawl into bed.

***

Over the next twelve months, the liturgical year looped around me, with work weekends and services swirling like snowflakes in a blizzard. I spent my Saturdays cleaning St. Xavier's chapel and then assisted the anointed sacristan at mass on Sundays. It was hard to keep up with the amount of work and harder still for me to shut off my brain when it came time to do it. The head sacristan, Sr. Catherine, enforced the order of obedience, where complying with an authority figure, even if their request made no sense, even if it was onerous and seemingly unnecessary, was the only way to please god. I would spend the next thirteen years under her supervision and felt the chafe marks of her rule on my spirit many times over.

The following spring, in my second postulant year, the Bishop anointed me as a fully ordained sacristan. In the main house chapel, I knelt on a kneeler, dressed in my alb, the white robe with a hood that I would wear now each time I served at the altar. After pouring water over my hands, the Bishop placed a purificator, the linen used to wipe the chalice after mass, between my palms. He looped the cincture (a knotted cord that I would wear around my waist) between my hands and around my wrists to symbolize my being bound to the service of the Lord. The cord released, the purificator removed, the Bishop then took chrism oil and poured it over my hands. He gently touched a consecrated host to my palms, with the warning that I was now the guardian of Christ, that god placed himself into my sinful hands, just like he had placed himself into the hands of his captors.

That same day ended with my rinsing mounds of linens three times to remove any microscopic particles of the sanctified host that may be stuck to them and then carrying the heavy buckets of water outside to dump onto the ground. The water was not permitted to enter the sewer system. The fairytale prince, if he was watching, didn't ride up with an offer of help. And as far as I knew, my future husband, the big JC, was still leaning up against the wall, his arms folded, shaking his head at my foolishness.

Sharon Downey

My Second "Job"

Back in the early eighties, there was a local catalog store called David Weiss. It sold appliances, jewelry, and electronics. Pre Amazon, it was the place to find many different things at decent prices. Shopping there one weekend with my mother, I was shocked to see one of the secretaries from the bank behind the counter. She was helping a man select a watch. When she saw me, her face froze. I quickly averted my eyes, acting as if I hadn't seen her. *What is she doing here?* The idea of someone that I worked with having a second job seemed so odd to me—and yet, why should it? It was the holiday season, and I suppose the woman was looking to make a little extra money. Neither of us mentioned my sighting of her when we saw each other again on Monday morning.

I had a second job as well, only I wasn't paid for it. Every weekend, I worked my ass off at church as a sacristan. On Saturdays, I would rise before six, no matter what the weather or how tired I was. In the winter, I would layer on clothes: sweatpants over jeans, a T-shirt, sweatshirt, and heavy hoodie, to protect me from the chilly cold in the unheated church. Summers would see me in as little clothing as possible, enough to maintain some semblance of decency. I'd drive through the winter darkness or the summer sunrise down Route 51 and stop at McDonalds for a breakfast sandwich and coffee. Yes, I was young and foolish enough to eat that crap, but I can guarantee you, I burned off the calories. Once at the church, I would fuss with the tricky lock on the basement door and enter, enveloped by either the freezing cold or the heat and humidity, depending on the season. I trudged upstairs to start work.

Every vowed member of the Chapter was required to go to the chapel, in whatever CRC house they found themselves, and first pay their respects to the Lord before speaking to anyone. The extent of my complying with this rule was to give the tabernacle on the wall a cursory nod before starting in on my work for the day. I was certainly no saint kneeling on the floor in prayerful ecstasy before the divine presence. I was all business. I had a job to do. Like a general going into battle, I soon developed a system of operation, one that allowed me to accomplish the tasks at hand in the shortest amount of time possible.

I pulled the rough linen bag from its hook, where all the dirty linens and vestments were stuffed, and emptied them into the buckets I needed to rinse them in before I laundered them. I had to lug the heavy buckets of water out the back door, down the steps, across the parking lot, and into a nearby field. I couldn't dump the water in the gravel and dirt parking lot that was in front of the cellar door, because Thomas had forbidden it. The water made swampy mud in the summer and quickly froze in the winter. I learned to use the least amount of water possible while still making sure the items were completely soaked. I had to rinse the linens in fresh water three times, so I would pour the used rinse water into an empty bucket to cut down on the number of trips outside to the field.

Once I had rinsed everything in the church's basement sink, I lugged the wet items over to Thomas's house and struggled with the recalcitrant lock on his basement door. The basement stunk of dampness and mildew. I was greeted by the careening wild madness of Thomas's damn dog, a Doberman mix, whom I had judged was certifiably insane. I would usually pick something up off the floor, a dirty sock or one of the dog's toys, and hurl it over his head. He would skitter and turn to go after it. I'd close him off at the end of the hallway by shutting a door that led to the stairwell upstairs.

Most weeks I had to empty both the washer and dryer of the family's laundry before I could put the linens and vestments in to wash. Once when I complained about this added step, Thomas asked why I didn't fold the dry clothes and put the wet laundry into the dryer. I stared at him as if he had lost his mind and said slowly, "I'm a sacristan, not your laundress," before turning on my heel and heading back to my work.

With the laundry started, I returned to the church and brought downstairs all of the brassware—censor, incense boat, holy water bucket, and candlesticks—to polish. All of the brassware was usually blackened with soot and grimy fingerprints. The sacristans used a mixture of kerosene, steel wool, a polishing product called Brasso, and plenty of elbow grease to shine the brass. Both the kerosene and Brasso stunk to high heaven and made a mess of your hands. I placed a clean rag on the counter in the basement to protect its surface and lined up the articles to be polished in order, the dreaded censor saved for last. Encrusted with grime from the smoking incense, it was the hardest item to clean.

After finishing the polishing, I would head back upstairs and clean the altar area, either by dusting all of the woodwork or washing it down with Murphy's Oil Soap, alternating those choices every other week. The tiny dressing room, where Thomas vested before mass, was located to the right of the altar. I dusted the furniture and swept the carpet. The sacristy, located to the left of the altar, a mere closet of a space, had to be tidied up, the window washed, and an inventory made of any supplies that were needed. I then had to pick up those supplies from the Mother House. Next I would go back to Thomas's house and remove the wet linens from the washer and place them in a clean plastic bag. I threw the vestments into in the drier.

I placed the wet linens in the fridge in the church basement so that I could iron them Sunday morning. After rinsing the smelly polishing rags and any rags I'd used to clean the woodwork three times, I would run them through the washer and drier. After vacuuming the altar area, setting the altar up for mass, and bringing the clean vestments from the house to the church, I'd survey my work, looking for any last details. Only then would I finally head for home, usually in the early afternoon. I never ate lunch or stopped to rest while at the church.

***

After a forty-minute ride, I would be home and could relax. Or perhaps not, depending on the emotional temperature of the house once I arrived. Sometimes storms brewed, or icy conditions prevailed. I would try to hunker down and ride them out. What I wanted physically was water, food, and rest. I was instead called upon to play cook, scullery maid, or tongue-lashing victim, depending on the state of the world that day. My mother's spinal stenosis and arthritic knees would flare up, making simple tasks painful. Her body's failures exacerbated her moods. When I was a young child, she and her mother had shared the household duties, and now that I was an adult, she expected the same from me. My father would sit in the living room, the television blaring, lost in his own world. Rarely could I come home and sink down onto my bed for a few moments of peace.

Sunday mornings, mass was at eleven. I would be at the church by nine, which meant I could sleep in until eight. I would iron the vestments and small linens while Thomas conducted bible study before mass. He insisted that I set up my ironing board in the back of the basement hall, telling me I needed to also hear the word. Oftentimes I was the first to arrive, and Thomas would amble over from his house, sit at his designated spot, and watch me work. He'd then thumb through his bible, looking for the text he would teach on that day. A half hour before show time, I would vest in my white alb and cincture and serve at the altar during mass. Then I would clean up and reset the altar before finally heading for home. This pattern went on week after week for almost ten years. The only time the head sacristan approved my taking "off" was when I was going out of town on vacation, was in the hospital, or when I was sent to an out-of-town house. No one ever took my place or filled in for me otherwise. I worked whether I was sick or well, whether I was tired or rested, whether I felt up to doing it or not.

Friends, superiors, and others repeatedly told me that I was "fortunate" I could devote the hours the work of a sacristan demanded because I lived at home. Everyone assumed my mother ran the household. No mention was ever made of my family's sacrifice or the guilt that ensued for me. No one knew of the tightrope I walked each and every time I went to the church and then came home, hoping against hope that the reception I would receive was better than the last, but seldom was. I was also encouraged to become a resident of the Mother House, but I viewed that option as a jail sentence. Leaving home to live on my own was also untenable. It would simply provide proof to my parents, particularly my mother, that she was right—I had chosen my god over them. So I struggled to keep both ends of a sinking ship afloat, and I paid the price physically, mentally, and spiritually.

By the time I made my professed vows, I no longer attended prayer meetings on Monday nights at St. Xavier's and by the later years of my professed life, I no longer went to Chapter meetings on Wednesday nights. My "selective" schedule met with ire on the part of some, and I ignored the complaints. I watched others be excused over and over again from their commitments, for reasons I didn't possess—a cranky husband or neglected children.

It was clear that I truly never was the Bride of Christ. In becoming a sacristan, I had committed myself to the role of the unloving yet guilty wife, who power-cleans the house and serves dinner on time, yet never shows affection for her husband, because she is not in love with him—and they both know it.

Sr. Catherine

I started full-time employment at age nineteen. I've had quite a few supervisors in the ensuing years. Some were cranky, some were kind, and some were unhinged. As with relatives, you usually cannot choose the people who supervise your work. Often it takes a lot of skill and sometimes just sheer dumb luck to influence the people who are in control of whether or not you stay employed. The old axioms my parents taught me—work hard, show up every day, and keep your nose clean—were beneficial in this regard to a point. It also paid to be a mind reader, a therapist (unlicensed), and occasionally someone who speaks truth to power.

None of my worldly bosses prepared me for how to handle Sr. Catherine, the head sacristan. She was difficult for me to read, as opaque as a heavily draped window. She frequently expressed the opinion that no one truly accepted her authority or had any respect for her. I remember how upset she became when overhearing one of us asking another sacristan, "Where is she?" the two knowing without saying her name who they were speaking about.

"I have a name," she shouted at them. "I am not 'SHE!'"

I would watch her nervously picking and fussing with items used for services, constantly worried that we would screw up. Things never went according to plan. Rehearse, plan, drill, go over every tiny detail—then the other shoe would drop, and midstream, a new idea would come flitting into the Bishop's head, and he would throw Sr. Catherine into panic mode.

Once, Sr. Catherine assigned me the job of holding the book of prayers for blessing the oils and water on Holy Saturday. She drilled me in how to hold it at just the right angle and height and to turn the pages quickly and silently. Frankly, I was surprised Sr. Catherine let me do the job. She allowed a few select sacristans to be near the Bishop during services, and I certainly wasn't one of them. I didn't comment on her choosing me or suggest that another sacristan be given the job; by then, I had learned just to go with it.

Of course, the entire order of the blessings was changed. The Bishop simply looked at me, then at the cluster of priests and deaconates around him, and said quietly, "I'm going over there." He pointed to the table of oils across the open space in front of the altar. I nodded to him, he nodded back, and out of the corner of my eye, I could see Sr. Catherine's horrified face. This was not the order of the service. But the man decided to do something different, and I merely followed along, opening the book to the set of prayers he needed, and we went on. Later, Sr. Catherine was still buzzing about it, the sudden change the Bishop had taken. What did it mean spiritually? Should the order of the service be changed for next year? I choked back the urge to break into laughter. The man decided he wanted to bless oils first, not the water. Maybe at the moment it just made more sense to him. Maybe there was nothing more to it than he felt it was expedient and would allow him to sit down faster. Or maybe he just wanted to make his head sacristan squirm a little.

I think it surprised Sr. Catherine that I did not behave in an obsequious manner toward her or any of the others in authority, including the Bishop. While I respected his office and the power of it, I saw the Bishop as a human being, capable of failure just as the rest of us. When he spoke to me, which was rare, I simply responded quietly and even had the audacity to tell him no, which in the CRC was almost heretical.

***

One Holy Week, Sr. Catherine found me in the antechapel with the Bishop. He came in unexpectedly, dressed in his nightgown, his hair in bedhead mode, while I was dusting the altar. He began moving flowers from spot to spot. "Do we have any more hyacinths?" he asked me.

"No, I'm sorry, this is all we have," I said.

He handed me two potted lilies. "These need water." I nodded my head. He continued to fuss a bit more. "Move another fan in here, please. That one is not big enough."

"I'll get another from across the street," I told him. He nodded his head absently and left the room through the door that led back to his row house. I turned to take the plants to the nearest sink and saw Sr. Catherine standing there gaping at me.

"Is everything all right?" she asked in strangled whisper.

"I think so. These are dry." I nodded at the plants in my hands. She continued to block the doorway, and I cocked my head, silently asking her if she wanted me to say something more. Her face regained its normal blankness, but I could sense that the idea that I could handle the Bishop's requests without getting flustered or upset seemed to shock her. Maybe it even stirred a flicker of envy.

***

Like the professed, sacristans had a retreat day as well, where we had to confess our faults against our sacristan commitment in a group culpa. Sr. Catherine sat in silent judgment of the event and listened to everyone list their sins. I took my turn at the kneeler and rattled off what I felt were my biggest stumbling blocks: fear, lack of devotion, the consuming need to just get it over with—whatever *it* was. I remained on the kneeler, waiting for any accusation Sr. Catherine wanted to make against me. She let me have it.

"Sr. Mary Joseph, we accuse you of disobedience against ourself and against the authority of our position as head sacristan."

I knelt on the kneeler, not looking at her, my face flushed with anger. My blood boiled because I knew her accusation was true, to a point. I knew she viewed my inability to let go and completely acquiesce to her authority as wrong. It was as if despite all the years of work, all the sacrifices I had made, I still fell short in her eyes because I had the audacity to use my mind and rely on my own judgment. I was obedient on the surface, not in my heart.

***

Much of the problem between Sr. Catherine and me came down to my role at St. Xavier's Chapel. She wanted me to take the responsibility for the work I performed there without her relinquishing any of her authority over the place. The authorities in the CRC saw St. Xavier's Chapel as an extension of the Mother House, making it fall under Sr. Catherine's purview. Every wedding, funeral, or Chapter service held there was my responsibility to prepare for because Sr. Catherine did not want to deal with Fr. Thomas. She wanted simply to show up, if necessary, to serve at the event. As a result, I found myself caught between the rock and the hard place of their two combating wills.

On one occasion, at a wedding, there was the usual piss-poor contingent of a choir. I was running around like a beheaded chicken, with a last-minute to-do list that seemed never ending, when Thomas told me to go sing with the choir. Knowing full well Sr. Catherine would hang me up to dry for this, I said, "You tell Sr. Catherine what you want me to do, and if you two agree, I'll do it."

He glowered at me. "I told you to sing."

I shook my head. "No, I'm here as a sacristan. I'm not a member of the music ministry or of the choir here. You will have to tell Sr. Catherine what I'll be doing. I'm not getting caught in the middle between the two of you." He glared at me and stomped off. I knew I had won that skirmish. What I wasn't winning was the ongoing battle between my various roles of sacristan, Chapter member, and member of Thomas's flock.

***

Things between Sr. Catherine and me came to a head one Palm Sunday, a few years after St.Xavier's chapel had closed. I didn't come to the Mother House the Saturday before to help set up. I knew I would get my ass handed to me for it. There is a long-standing joke in my family about our last name and how the only time anyone ever yelled it on a job site or in an office was when we had the audacity to not show up for work. I think the joke actually started when my father stayed on the job while having a heart attack. No one noticed anything, until the next day when my father didn't show up for work.

I knew there would be a full crew of sacristans from out of town, and frankly I was dreading another "Hell Week," as I called them. I tried to contact Sr. Catherine, both at home and at the Mother House, but was unable to reach her. I stayed home that Saturday, and on Sunday, I showed up for the service. It was a lovely morning, the kind of spring day in late April that makes your heart ache, as they are so rare. Brilliant sunshine, warm temperatures, every tree in full blossom. What made the heartache worse was that I had resigned myself to spend the entire day indoors. I slipped up the side stairs, peeked into the rapidly filling first floor to take a cursory glance at the tabernacle, and turned to head down to the basement to dress in my alb and cincture. Waiting for me on the landing leading to the downstairs hall was Sr. Catherine. "Where were you yesterday?" she demanded. I stopped in my tracks, eyeing her. She was not given to histrionics; she generally kept a tight rein on herself. Her weapon of choice with me in the past was cutting coldness, not blazing anger.

Clustered on the stairs were some of the out-of-towners. They lined up to process outside in front of the Temple, where they would wave their palm fronds and sing, as if welcoming Christ into Jerusalem. Some of them eyed me warily, as if I had suddenly grown a second head or had some type of contagious pox. Others smiled faintly, as if taking comfort in the fact that it was someone else, not them, who was under attack.

"I called here several times. I wasn't able to get through to you on the phone. I had told you last week that I probably would not be able to come yesterday." I managed to keep my voice quiet and even, despite my desire to scream.

"You were disobedient. We had all of this setup to do and virtually no help. You are not permitted to vest today." Sr. Catherine glared at me, her face blotchy and red, her chin set in defiance.

The background noise—people clamoring, voices calling to one another, excited children screaming, babies crying—droned on. I glanced around to see pity reflected in some of the faces closest to me. My lack of a response made Sr. Catherine squirm a bit as she grasped and stroked the crucifix that lay on her chest. I kept silent, my eyes fixed on hers. If she believed I was going to break down, beg for her forgiveness, and plead to serve at the altar, she was sadly mistaken. I pulled my shoulders back, straightened my spine, gave her a brief nod, turned around, and walked back up the stairs and out the side door, back into the brilliant sunshine. I knew I would spend the upcoming days working long hours. I made my decision. I was going home. I'd had enough.

The fact was, there had been plenty of help to setup on Saturday, but Sr. Catherine undoubtedly had excused the out-of-town sacristans—and most likely, some of the Mother House sacristans as well—to go to the Cantata practice, where the story of Christ is reenacted on the stage. Her workhorse had stayed home. I walked to my car and calmly drove away. When I arrived home, the house was empty, my parents having gone to mass. I called my Chapter superior's home and spoke to her mother. "Could you please ask Irene to call me, Mrs. O'Donahue? I want to explain why I left mass today."

"Oh, sure, sure. Are you feeling unwell?" Mrs. O'Donahue was a kind woman, whom Sr. Irene, my superior, would often accuse jokingly of "playing Mother Superior."

"No, I'm fine," I said. "I just…well, I had a little altercation with Sr. Catherine."

Mrs. O'Donahue tutted. "Oh, well, I'm sure it's just a misunderstanding. All of you sacristans work too hard! Now, don't worry. I'll let Margaret Ann (this was Sr. Irene's birth name) know you called. You take care."

When my parents came home, they were surprised but also delighted. I told my mother what had happened, and she quickly became incensed. "And you'll be there this week to all hours of the night and this is what you get? That woman (my mother could never remember names) is just pissed because she knows you'll work yourself sick, and most of the others won't lift a finger."

Later, my superior, Sr. Irene, called me and commiserated. "I'm just sorry that she treated you that way, Mary Joseph, and that she drove you away from god's house."

"I was too upset to stay there, Irene. I know that I shouldn't have reacted that way, but, well, honestly, this has been coming for a while now."

"I know, I know. Frankly, I see what goes on. Sr. Catherine leans on a few of you sacristans way too much, and there are others who don't put in the time they can and should."

I sighed. "I have SWF syndrome, I guess."

"SWF?" Irene asked, puzzled.

"Single White Female. You know, no life, no problems, and all the time in the world." Irene and I both laughed. She was in pretty much the same boat as me. She worked full time, lived with her mother, and had no responsibilities—or so everyone told us.

"Listen, you know, Sr. Maria Faustina is counsel for the Priesthood. You need to call her and tell her exactly what you told me." I agreed, and Irene wished me well. "Don't let this get you down!" she told me. I contacted Sr. Maria Faustina later that evening. After she listened to me relate the episode with Sr. Catherine, she sighed.

"Well, Sr. Catherine had no business dressing you down in public like that."

"I just feel she could have pulled me aside and let me know privately that she was not happy with me."

"I agree. And I also agree with Sr. Irene, about how Sr. Catherine leans on certain individuals in the sacristan program too heavily. I'll speak to her about this. Don't worry about it further."

When I saw Sr. Catherine the following Wednesday evening, she approached me and asked that we step into the dressing room used by the sacristans. "We would like to ask your forgiveness for what we said to you on Sunday," she began. I heard the words, but my eyes focused on hers—and there was no contrition present there. I had done the one thing that would make her truly angry—I had gone over her head. I raised a hand.

"Please, there's no need. We'll start over, shall we?" I had made my point and that was enough for me. I simply wasn't going to allow her to step on me anymore. She nodded and we left the room.

***

When I made the decision not to renew my vows on my ten-year anniversary of profession, I didn't discuss the matter with Sr. Catherine. As head sacristan, she would receive a list of those renewing their vows, and my name would not appear on the list. I had no desire to listen to any arguments from her on why I should renew. Then again, I had my doubts as to her opposing my decision at all. One weekend before the renewal service, I bent over an ironing board in the Temple basement, pressing vestments. Sr. Catherine and I were alone.

"Mary Joseph, are you intending to renew your vows?" I looked at her, a woman who had forever been a thorn in my side. It was as if a bright light fastened itself on her, and I finally saw her as she truly was—a woman much like me, tired, overworked, burdened. I also knew that I couldn't help her, because I needed to help myself.

"No," I replied quietly and bent my head back over my work. She made no comment. We never spoke of my decision again. Did she fault herself or the endless work of the sacristans as factoring into my choice? Or was she thinking that she, too, would like to walk away, start over again, leave the vowed life behind? Our relationship was not one that allowed questions like these; they remained unasked and unanswered.

All True Vows

Hell Week

I've never worked in retail, but friends and family have told me about the horrors of working Black Friday sales. They've told me of having to unpack endless boxes of sale items, moving goods off the floor to make room for gift displays, and dealing with hordes of angry, pushy customers. I've heard stories about customers fighting with each other and store personnel over merchandise, prices, coupons, and gift-wrapping. Many of the people relating these stories quit their retail jobs in disgust over this long weekend of crass consumerism. I've known store managers who've worked eighty- to one-hundred-hour weeks, some sleeping in the store's employee lounge for snatches of time so that the work could be finished.

Sacristans had their own version of the Black Friday weekend—Holy Week, or Passion Week as some refer to it. Over time, I learned to call Holy Week "Hell Week." Of course, I had to watch when and to whom I used that term. Many agreed with me, but few dared speak it aloud. The week actually started the Saturday before Palm Sunday with the daylong practices for the Cantata. On stage, a cast enacted the life story of Christ, complete with a simulated crucifixion scene. The choir sang in the background with appropriate hymns. Everyone in Chapter was expected to do something for the Cantata, whether that was to sing, act, help dress actors backstage, work with props and lighting, sell raffle tickets, or be an usher. The whole thrust of the performance was the altar call, when the Bishop would go to the podium and call people to give their souls to Christ. The CRC promoted the annual Cantata as its one big outreach event for souls.

But as the years passed, I couldn't help but notice the same people returned for the performance year after year, like those who go to see the *Nutcracker* every holiday season, simply because they have always done so. The message the Bishop preached regarding the Cantata was always the same—if one soul came to Christ because of our efforts, it was worth it.

My first two years in Chapter, I sang in the choir for the Cantata performance and spent the Saturday before Palm Sunday in the daylong rehearsals. Once I was an anointed sacristan, I was required to spend that Saturday prepping for the Palm Sunday service. We decorated the altar with fresh palm fronds artfully arranged in sand-filled urns. We prepared additional palms to be blessed and distributed. After the mass on Palm Sunday, I would stay behind and find a quiet place to hide out or spend my time checking the house chapels, waiting for the Cantata to be over so that I could be excused to go home.

Palm Sunday was just the start of a very long week. On Monday and Tuesday, we set up the antechapel, a place where the only tabernacle would be located after the Holy Thursday Mass. The sacristans decorated the small room, usually used as an office, with Easter flowers and a multitude of candles. It was steamy and stifling, like a hothouse—even in the years when Easter fell early and the outside air was cold.

Wednesday was Spy Wednesday, the day the Bishop had taught the Chapter that Christ was actually crucified. He had lain in the grave for three days and three nights until Sunday. The Chapter read the Passion aloud. One of the sacristans would take the lectionary down the aisles of the Chapter, while another followed with a candle. Everyone who was seated held lit tapers, and as Chapter members read the passages aloud, those sitting around the reader extinguished their tapers. As we moved along with the book, the whole Chapter fell into darkness. The Bishop read the last section of the Passion, and at the words "and He gave up the ghost," the sacristans swung wooden clackers, and the office books of the Chapter were slammed shut almost in unison. It was an eerie sound in the darkness. The Bishop and the priests stripped the altar, striking its edges with a cincture. The Bishop then smacked all the corners of the altar with a lectionary; then holding the book over his head, he dropped it right on the middle of the altar. The sacristans and deaconates dressed the altar with flickering candles. Over a large pillow, they draped a purple chasuble, a vestment the priests wore that represented the seamless tunic of Christ. On the pillow, they placed a large crucifix.

The Chapter then left in silence—save for the sacristans, who spent the night redressing the altars in each house and chapel and removing the purple coverings—which encased all of the statues—and exchanging them for white ones. This had to be done overnight, so that when the Bishop awoke the next day, everything was ready for the Chrism mass on Thursday evening. Thursday started early, with loads of laundry, endless ironing of vestments and linens, and the setup for the foot-washing service to be held late that evening.

Also on Thursday, the sacristans emptied every tabernacle in all of the houses of consecrated hosts. The only communion wafers available for Good Friday would be those consecrated at the Holy Thursday Mass. This led to a mass consumption of the consecrated bread, until you could scarcely eat anymore. We would go looking for people to help in the mission of finishing off the last of the wafers. The Priesthood and the Bishop celebrated Holy Thursday mass with great solemnity, for it was the night that Christ confirmed and established the priesthood. All of the Priesthood, even the sacristans, received an anointing that night. Afterwards, the Chapter ate the Pesach meal, complete with unleavened bread.

The work continued after dinner on Thursday for the Good Friday services, where everyone wore black, including black albs, all of which had to be laundered and pressed. All the chapels were now barren; the tabernacles were left open, for the Lord was now in the hands of those who would take his life. The sacristans stripped the altars in each house and thoroughly cleaned each chapel.

Friday started early, with laundry, ironing of vestments, and prepping for the Friday night vigil service. The sacristans could only redress the main house altar after noon on Friday. There was no mass on Friday, but a communion service was held at three. The priests distributed the hosts that had been consecrated at the Holy Thursday mass. Deaconates read a long list of prayers, with the litany "Let us kneel, let us stand" in between each set. Every type of sinner was prayed for, even the Jews who were blamed for taking Christ's life.

After the communion service, everyone would come down the center aisle and prostrate themselves on the floor three times, once for the world, once for sinners, and the last time for oneself. The deaconates placed a crucifix under the altar, flanked by two burning candles. Carefully, so as not to catch your clothes on fire, each person was to kiss the five wounds on the crucifix. We then had a meatless supper. Friday was the longest night. We had to finish the remaining cleaning, redress the altars, and prepare for the arrival of the Risen Lord in the form of the Holy Saturday host. A pyx in each tabernacle contained an Easter Host as the true presence until the next Easter.

Deaconate men set up tables in front of the altar with the Paschal candles, jugs of oils, and vats full of spring water ready to be sanctified. We sacristans ran on caffeine and sugar. One of the priests would excuse us from the Lenten fast, and junk food would magically appear. After we finished all of the cleaning, polishing, and setting up, Sr. Catherine would go over the order of the service for the next day. I was usually so exhausted by then that I wanted to cry. I finally left to go home at 3:00 a.m., knowing I had to be back at church by 8:00 a.m. Too wired to sleep, I can remember one year sitting at home in the kitchen in the middle of the night, eating slices of homemade nut roll slathered in butter. My mother trailed down from her bed to stand there and shake her head at me. I cut off some more of the cake and ate it.

"You're not supposed to be eating that," she remarked wryly, probably secretly pleased. She found the whole fasting thing ridiculous.

"I don't give a damn." I shoved more of the cake in my mouth. I stumbled up the stairs to bed and tossed and turned until it was time to get up again and start the madness anew.

Saturday was essentially Easter Sunday for the Chapter. The Bishop brought in the new fire, lit the new Paschal candle, and then went on to bless all of the oils and water. The new hosts were consecrated at mass, and the out-of-towners scrambled afterwards to retrieve their boxes of candles, bags of oil bottles, jugs of holy water, and the pyx containing the Host to take back to their home chapels. The scene after mass was utter chaos, with deaconates assigned to fill and distribute oil and water bottles, and people picking up their baskets of Easter food that had been blessed. Each house and chapel at the

Mother House had to have the Host re-installed in its tabernacle by a deaconate accompanied by a sacristan going before them with a lit seven-day vigil light and ringing a set of bells.

During the years I spent at St. Xavier's Chapel, this day was an even longer one for me. I had to drive to the church as if the hounds of hell were after me so that I would have time to completely clean and polish everything in the chapel and get everything ready for mass before Thomas arrived with the Easter host. He of course had little or no patience and threatened to give me only a fifteen-minute head start. I felt like I was in a marathon I was bound to lose. I would beg Grace to delay him with a long story about some recent tragedy or else pick a fight with him, the latter definitely guaranteeing me more time; he could never resist another opportunity to say he was right about something. Fortunately, Thomas's threat never held water. In about an hour, after accomplishing some of the work that I would normally take hours to do on a Saturday morning, I would take a lit censor and greet Thomas and the Easter host at the back door of the chapel. He would put the host in the tabernacle, and we would sing and praise the returning Lord. Then Easter Sunday would mean going out early to the church, finishing the laundry, and serving mass. In later years, when St. Xavier's had closed, I took Easter Sunday off to rest and recover.

The pageantry and spiritual significance of the events of Holy Week were lost to me in the endless rounds of cleaning, ironing, setting up, and tearing down. The sacristans were the servants of the servants of god, but in not taking time to feel or to acknowledge the solemnity of the rites we performed, the experiences became for me blank and meaningless. What joy I took from those days came from the shared experience with others who worked alongside me.

Sharon Downey

Thank You for Being a Friend

In fourth grade, my all-white elementary school was integrated. Kids from a neighboring all-black school transferred to my school. Among them was a tall, self-assured girl my age named Marguerite. Her skin was the color of a café au lait, and her voice was a rich contralto. We found out we shared a birthday and became inseparable. She was smart and confident. I made her laugh. For the next two years, we were best friends—then junior high school happened. We moved to another school, which combined all of the six elementary schools in our district. Marguerite, or Maggie as she was called, found new friends, while I went adrift. It was the first time I realized that changed circumstances could make or break friendships. High school brought more change, with the various cliques of the "burnouts" and party girls. I settled in with a few outcasts like myself, who didn't fit into any one group.

After high school, I went to business school for nine months. There I was exposed to people I probably would never have hung out with in high school. I met the country girls gone wild who had never spent time in a big city, and I met older women looking to revamp their skills for the job market. In my first job at the bank, I met another cast of characters—some of them worthy of their own reality television shows, with drama and flair to spare. Often people become friends when necessity throws them together. I was fortunate that I had people who made the time I spent in the CRC a bit easier. From each of them, I learned lessons that have stayed with me.

Grace's friend, Annie, became one of my closest and dearest friends. She had been born with a spinal condition that caused her head to practically rest on her shoulders. She almost lacked a neck. She had wild, curly red hair and a voice so thick and deep that my mother nicknamed her "Gravel Gertie." She was kind and hard-working. And she called a spade a spade. I don't really remember anyone calling her by her sister name, Madeline. Annie ran the cleaning ministry at Clairton, taking care of the entire place with very little help. She mowed the huge lawns in summer and rented a carpet cleaner, using her own money, to care for the church floor. Annie later joined the sacristan training program for a short time and helped me to care for the altar, and she served at mass. She was generous to a fault, always giving to help others. I found out later that she bought her class superior's office books for her because the woman could not afford them. Annie showed me the difference between loyalty and blind commitment.

Paula was another of the St. Xavier gang. She was pretty, with soft facial features and a wild laugh. No one called her Paula, everyone used her last name, Cullen. Even after she took her novice step and chose the name Sister Margaret Marie, none of us called her that; she was still Cullen. The two of us made a wild trip one summer to Myrtle Beach, driving down to South Carolina in her beat-up Chevy. I paid for the hotel and didn't find out till we arrived that Paula had virtually no money for the trip. She wanted to go back to the place she had spent time while vacationing with Thomas and his extended family. It was a pilgrimage of sorts for her. I stayed under the umbrellas near the pool, while Paula walked around and around the house that Thomas had rented. Paula was enamored with Thomas. She even volunteered to clean his house for him, an offer he accepted without blinking an eye—after all, he was her spiritual director. I felt sorry for Paula. At the same time, she ticked me off, too. She was too bright, I thought, too good-hearted to allow Thomas to use her that way. I learned from her to trust my own inner bullshit detector.

Tracy was Paula's neighbor. They lived in the same apartment building. Paula brought her to a prayer meeting, and Tracy found a home in the church. Tracy had a fragility about her, a soft neediness that men found attractive, including Thomas. I chose her to be my maid of honor when I made my novice step. While I was close to her,

I still held back a bit. I was plain and ordinary; Tracy was exotic and special. She could be crying her eyes out, mascara running down her cheeks, using a sock to wipe snot from her face, and people would still be attracted to her. We went to Florida on a week's vacation with my parents—or I should say, we attempted to go to Florida, save for a small event called the Blizzard of Ninety-Three. We spent the night at the airport. Our charter did not cancel our flight, and we assumed we would be leaving. Shortly after arriving at the airport, the authorities shut it down. The governor declared a state of emergency and ordered everyone to stay off the roads. We were trapped. Tracy spent most of her time in the airport bar, drinking bottles of water so that she could smoke a cigarette. My mother was appalled. "You didn't tell me she smoked!" she hissed at me as Tracy took off yet again. We eventually made the trip the following year. It wasn't a ringing success. I felt caught between my parents and my friend, trying to please everyone and failing miserably on both sides. Years later, our relationship fell apart when Tracy began to date the still-married Thomas. My reaction to her newfound love affair was to shut her out of my life. Tracy gave me the hardest lesson I needed to learn—to give others the benefit of the doubt and not simply freeze them out of my life.

When I entered the sacristan training program, I found myself spending most of my time with my fellow trainees and the anointed sacristans who were my teachers. Sr. Janet was one of my favorites among the sacristans. She was of the old school, those who had joined the Chapter in its early days—when things were much more difficult, penances flung around like confetti, requirements much more tightly enforced. Once beautiful, she was still luminous. Her razor-thin body, whittled by hard work and sorrow, had become a holy and humble vessel for her spirit, which blazed from her eyes. I was both in awe of her and scared to death of her; I definitely did not want to disappoint her. We traveled together one weekend to the church, Blessed Sacrament, in Crawford County, Pennsylvania, for a wedding. We worked together to clean and decorate the church. Later, during the ceremony, I found myself watching Janet, her face radiant, obviously happy to be there to share and witness the joy of the young couple. One of the darkest moments in Janet's life came when her son committed suicide. During the funeral mass, all of us watched as she carefully laid the embroidered pall on the casket and smoothed it with her hands, as if tucking in her child one last time. My own cares and concerns, particularly with my health, seemed so small in comparison. Janet's courage in the face of such sorrow was her gift to me.

Sr. Rachel was a young mother, who spent much of her time working on sacristan tasks from home. Her beautiful calligraphy was showcased on all of the labels, place cards, and certificates the CRC issued. Occasionally she was able to be present, working the later shifts of the Holy Week work details, while her husband, a second deaconate, stayed home with the children. She was one of the most organized people I'd ever met. Her traveling bag carried all of her calligraphy and stationary supplies, plus snacks—in case her kids needed something. She was good-natured and fun to be around. She contracted lung cancer and died when she was just forty years old; everyone was devastated. I dreamt about her after her death, seeing her with her back facing me as she held a golden-haired child. Rachel showed me that life is fleeting, mysterious, and precious.

Among my Chapter classmates was Karen, a divorced mother with grown children. Karen, later Sr. Priscilla, also joined the sacristan program and became a resident of the Mother House. She had tried Chapter once before and had left, she told me, because it wasn't the right time. She had red hair and a hearty laugh, and always spoke with no filter; what she thought immediately passed her lips. When the CRC began a school in Africa, Karen applied to be sent there as a missionary. The CRC selected her to go, and I remember how excited she was. She soon understood how difficult things were in this part of the world and how little control the CRC could exert over what happened there. It was a hard time for her. Karen returned to the states and decided she would not go back to Africa. She told me later that the Bishop was upset with her for her decision, but she made up her mind and then left the CRC for good. Karen showed me her courage, even though I doubt she would think of herself as courageous.

Julie was eighteen years old when she and I took our aspirant step. I was twenty-six and could not imagine knowing what I wanted at eighteen as she seemed to know. She was bright and vivacious. In some ways, she reminded me of playful puppy or kitten that everyone found adorable and doted upon. Julie or Sr. Julie Lauren as she became later, studied to be a nurse and then also joined the sacristan program. She helped care for some of the older, infirm members of the Chapter, spending hours just talking to them. Later, Julie was engaged to be married, and I found myself going with her one Saturday afternoon to look at bridesmaid dresses. Her family was far away in New Jersey, and she wanted someone to accompany her. She convinced me to try on a dress so she could see what it looked like on a body. When I exited the dressing room, she said, "You look beautiful! You have to be in my wedding!" Crushed in a hug, I acquiesced. It was several years, an abandoned first engagement, and another groom later that I fulfilled that pledge to her. She gave me the gift of being in the moment, every moment.

    I was fortunate and blessed to have these wonderful women in my life. Those mentioned here and so many more, each in their own way, helped me to weather the storms that arose in my life and made my time in the CRC much more bearable. I can only hope that I was able to give them some gifts in return. I owe a debt of gratitude to all of them.

Novice Step

Wearing a uniform was something very foreign to me. Educated in the public schools, I wasn't used to rules on what to wear, save that my clothing cover certain body parts. I never joined the Brownies or the Girl Scouts. I didn't become a nurse or doctor, with the obligatory white coat. No military service meant I never wore Army green or Navy blue. My novice step in my religious life, however, would set me apart from everyone else in the world. I would dress in a distinct and very different way. The novice step in Chapter occurred in the fourth year of the five-year novitiate and was the time when we received our first brown garb. Not only would I look different, I would hence forth be known by a different name, not the one my parents had chosen for me, but one I chose within the confines outlined by the novice mistress. For Chapter members, assimilation was expected—no, it was demanded. As part of the vow of poverty, we had to extract and toss out any desire or longing for individuality before taking the novice step. Like a line of paper dolls, we would be indistinguishable from one another. We would answer to new names, chosen from models of piety and virtue.

About six weeks before the step, we were separated from the Chapter and sent to the back rows of the hall where we had started out as aspirants. My classmates and I were now known as "No-Name" Smith or Jones or whatever our last name was. The professed took delight in saying things like "Oh, look, here comes one of the No-Names." We were in one of those between places again, and someone jokingly remarked that we best not die before the novice service, or on our tombstone would be written, "Here lies No-Name Smith, who lost their name and never got a new one."

***

Sr. Hedwig, the novice mistress, gathered my class together one Wednesday night to teach us about the taking of our new names. We each had to choose two names. The first was of the saint we wanted to emulate and fashion ourselves after; the second was of the saint whom we wanted to pray for us, to help us keep our vows. No other Chapter member could have our name, nor could we take the same name as any other member, living or deceased. Just like our Chapter number, our name was to be unique.

I had chosen my sister name on the day of my aspirant step. In the heady rush of that day, when I still believed I could persevere in this vowed life, I decided I wanted to be Sr. Mary Joseph. The novice mistress told us that, like a Jewish bride, we would take our husband's name before our own so that all of us were Sr. Jesus X X or Br. Jesus X X. My name would be Jesus Mary Joseph. Every written communication in the Chapter was sealed at the top with the initials JMJ and a tiny +. I chose the names of the Holy Family. I still clung to my need to "save" my family. That was the reason I remained in Chapter, I told myself. I felt by taking the name Mary Joseph, I was giving god the hint to make certain I would not be separated from my family in the hereafter. After all, I now knew that just going to church every week like my parents did wasn't enough; they had to be born again, accept Christ into their hearts, and live lives committed to Christ. Like my beloved Baba, who prayed endless rosaries to limit the suffering of her darling husband in purgatory, I was going to make sacrifices to pay for the "insurance policy" for my family. I told myself this neat white lie to seal up the gaping hole in my logic.

Then the boom fell. Sr. Hedwig announced that the Bishop had decided that we were to be the "Class of Martyrs," and so the sister or brother names we took had to be those of martyr saints. My heart sunk. Good Saint Joseph was not a martyr—far from it. In Catholic catechism class, my teachers taught that St. Joseph was the patron saint of a good death; he died quietly, with Jesus and Mary beside him. Sr. Hedwig had told us that Mary was the Queen of Martyrs; her heart "had been pierced with the sword" at the crucifixion, so the first part of my name was secure. I suppose my face showed my disappointment because Jim, our class superior, asked me what was wrong.

"I can't have the name I want," I said quietly. "St. Joseph wasn't a martyr."

He shook his head. "No, but you could probably find a saint whose name was Joseph, who was a martyr. Don't give up yet." I smiled. He was a conniver, and I liked him for that.

The internet was still a pie-in-the-sky dream in 1990. I went to Hillman Library on the University of Pittsburgh campus and found a copy of *Butler's Lives of the Saints*. In the back was an alphabetical listing. I found a Chinese catechist named Joseph Tshang-ta-Pong, who was martyred on my birthday. He was at that time only beatified (the church later canonized him in 2000), but that was enough to get my name. I copied the single page on him and wrote my submission on why I was choosing these saints' names for my sister name.

It wasn't until much later that I saw the irony of belonging to the "Class of Martyrs." At least in my case, I was already one. I had to sacrifice, give, serve, and bend over backwards in order for god to see me. It mirrored the relationship I had with my earthly father, a man whose fears and inability to show love, drove me, in part, to offer myself to a god who I felt was much like him.

***

A few weeks before Investiture, which is the weekend set of services for the people making steps in the novitiate, the seamstresses delivered the garb for my class to the Mother House. For the women, it consisted of a brown skirt and tunic, which we wore over a white blouse, long or short sleeved, depending on the season, and a silver crucifix on a chain. We had to purchase a pair of brown shoes. For the women, the shoes had to be low heeled. For the service, the women were also responsible for purchasing a white, long-sleeved blouse, and we had to bring our blouse and shoes in to show Sr. Hedwig before the service.

Sr. Hedwig picked up my shoes from the box and studied them. "Real leather," she murmured. She looked at the label inside. "And they're Clarks. Those are expensive."

I reddened. My size-five feet were difficult to shod and I was used to spending a good bit of money on shoes. I said nothing, but she could see the embarrassment in my face. She smiled and put them back. "Well, you'll have them for a while, which is good." She traced her fingers over the collar of the blouse and looked at the tag. "Kaufmann's?" she asked. The local department store wasn't exclusive, but it certainly wasn't a bargain basement either.

I nodded. "But it was on sale."

She didn't respond. She put the blouse under a tunic to make certain that the collar wasn't so big that it covered up too much of the garb. She nodded her head and placed the items to the side. I passed the inspection.

The women wore the same triangular white veil we'd worn for the past three years, only with three red-stitched crosses now, one over each ear and one at the point over our spine, with a brown strip of fabric sewn across the top. The men wore brown shirts with hoods attached, the same silver crucifix as the women, and brown slacks. The cross on the top of their white skullcaps was now brown. The women's tunic and skirt were made of a heavy polyester fabric, uncomfortably hot in the summer and impossible to keep clean. The weave of the fabric easily trapped dirt. Sr. Hedwig told us that, like our veils, we needed to rinse our new garb once, dumping the water onto the ground before washing the garments in the laundry.

***

The day of the service, we wore white clothes again, as we had for each of our previous two steps. I had kept the same outfit from my aspirant and postulant steps so that I didn't have to go shopping for something new. Maybe I should have pointed out that bit of poverty to Sr. Hedwig, but then, that would have been the sin of pride. Over the floor in front of the altar, the sacristans spread a pall, a white sheet-like cloth. One by one, deaconates led us in and then helped us first to kneel and then to lie face down on the pall. With so many of us, we had to space ourselves strategically so that we all fit. Standing around the outside edges of the pall were all of our bridesmaids and best men, the people we had chosen to be the witnesses of our commitment to god. Best men and bridesmaids prayed for the sister or brother who had chosen them and carried the responsibility of reminding them when they fell short in keeping their vows.

The sacristans brought out a second pall that they had folded in a fan fold. The bridesmaids and best men passed the cloth from hand to hand until they held it up over us like an unfurled flag. One of the sacristans snapped her fingers, and the bridesmaids and best men lowered the cloth on top of us and left us to rest there, sandwiched between the two pieces of cloth. This represented our shroud as we laid down our lives to rise up with Christ.

Depending on the mood of the Bishop, the cloth was left over us for as long as he indicated. At another snap of a finger, our bridesmaids and best men lifted the top cloth, held it above us again, and then gently lowered it back down.

I kept my face pillowed in my arms, feeling the pull of my lower back. I had heard stories from older Chapter members of how they had had mystical experiences under the pall, how they had seen deceased family members or heard the voices of angels. I simply wanted to get up off the floor. My wanting to have a mystical experience was part of my needy nature, and complaints of this spiritual dryness in the past had earned me scoldings and penances from the novice mistress. She told me we were to suffer with the dryness, offer up the difficulty for our sins, and not seek immersion in signs and gifts of the Spirit. I lay there on the floor, holding my breath in an effort to keep still. I was doing what I had done my entire life—seeking approval, seeking healing from the woundedness of my heart, seeking to remain small and out of sight.

At another click, the bridesmaids and best men lifted the pall and folded it quickly. One by one, deaconates helped us up from the floor and then lowered us to kneel on a pillow in front of the Bishop. He handed each of us our garb and said, "Divest yourself of the things of this world and clothe yourself in the habit of St. Francis." Some of my class members, slain in the spirit, had to then be helped or in some cases carried up the steps to the second floor, where we were to dress with the help of our bridesmaid or best man.

I managed to get up the steps under my own steam, with my bridesmaid, Tracy, trailing after me. I got dressed quickly, and she straightened my veil and my crucifix on its chain around my neck. Despite the heat, we both wore long-sleeved blouses and gloves. The elastic band that held up my new garb skirt dug into my waist. "You look beautiful," Tracy said, smiling. I felt strange. I told myself it would take some time getting used to wearing this outfit.

My class exited outside through a side door and processed back into the house, where we knelt on the floor in two straight rows. Beside each of us stood our bridesmaid or best man placing one hand on our right shoulder and holding in the other our Paschal candle, which bore one frankincense nail. We read our vows together, each of us in turn calling out our new sister or brother names. We then went one by one to the Bishop to receive a blessing, and the service was over.

Sr. Hedwig had told us before the service that this was the pivot point for many people in their Chapter walk. The idea of wearing clothing that set them apart, more than just a simple triangular veil or small skullcap, would cause some to jettison the whole idea of taking vows. We were different and wore that difference now into the world. It was another test. Before heading home at night on Wednesdays, I removed my tunic, crucifix, and veil, leaving myself as just an ordinary woman in a white blouse and brown skirt. I wasn't fooling anyone except myself. I had moved further away from who I was into a world that would continue to demand greater and greater sacrifices from me.

All True Vows

The Retreat

When I was in middle school, a round of slumber parties sprang up overnight. Seemed everyone I knew was inviting people to come over, eat bad-for-you food, play silly games, and try not to fall asleep, which really took the word "slumber" completely out of the equation. I was one of those kids (and still am as an adult) who couldn't fall asleep in a strange place anyways, so I was the perfect sleepover guest. Each of these non-sleeping events had their own rituals—black lighting, games like treasure hunts and telling scary stories, and the inevitable ice cube down someone's back who'd had the temerity to fall asleep.

At the midpoint of my second novice year, I was off to a week-long slumber party, only the rules were very different—no games but plenty of prayer, no black lighting but plenty of candle light, and no ice cubes but lots of self-accusation and pointing out other's faults. I looked forward to this retreat about as much as a root canal without anesthesia. The idea of being cooped up with strangers—with nothing to do except pray and accuse myself of sin—was not only frightening but also life threatening to my overactive merciless ego. Not being busy, not having anything to do, not being productive—what kind of cruel mastermind came up with this form of senseless torture? My inner "girl with the clip board" would rag me to death.

The silent retreat was held in the summer in the mission house, an old barn of a building, rickety and musty smelling, located across the street from the main buildings of the Mother House. We could choose which week we would attend. I chose the first one, proving once again that I am my mother's child. Whenever she was faced with a situation that was potentially daunting or painful, her go to response was, "Let's get this over with." I asked for time off at work, without telling anyone where I was going. I wasn't sure how I could even explain it.

Yeah, I'm going to be locked up in a house in a bad section of town for a week with three other women and two men. We won't be allowed to talk to each other, but we will be praying. Uh-huh.

In fact, I never told people I worked with about my life in Chapter. I wasn't Grace; I could never imagine telling anyone about how I spent my weekends. My fear of judgement was too strong. I wasn't willing to be the "crazy" person who talked about religion all of the time. Thomas, Catherine, and the others gave me flak for this—particularly when it came to fundraising. I should have been willing to sell the raffle tickets, the crafts, and the food items because this would give me an opportunity to "witness" for god. "If you are ashamed of Christ, he will be ashamed of you before his father," they told me. My worlds ran on separate tracks. I had my home life, my work life, my school life, and my religious life. I worked to keep those tracks from crossing each other—with varying degrees of success.

I was terrified about the retreat. Nothing I'd had to do thus far in my religious life scared me as much. I'd have no escape, no place to hide, no work to throw myself into. I'd have only my classmates, myself, and god.

***

I arrived on Saturday night and parked my car on the street so I would be able to see it from the upstairs chapel windows of the house. I wondered if it would be safe. On previous occasions, others had been stolen. Sr. Hedwig, our novice mistress, met us at the side door. The altar was set for mass, with a kneeler in front, and chairs were lined up in Chapter order. A tabernacle sat front and center on the altar. "You are not held prisoner here," she said. "The door is not locked to keep you in, but to keep the world out. You may leave at any time, and no one will hold it against you."

A furtive glance around me revealed hollow expressions. I could just imagine the gossip: *Hey, did you hear about Sr. So and So? Yep, ran* screaming into the street after the first night of the retreat. I knew she wouldn't make it!

Sr. Hedwig then went over the order of the day. We would start with the Office of Readings at three o'clock in the morning and wrap up at eight in the evening with communion and night prayers. We were to remain in silence at all times save for prayers and culpa. We were to wear our full garb for all prayers, culpa, and mass; otherwise street clothes were OK. "What you get out of this week will be what you put into it," Sr. Hedwig said. "The Lord wants to work with you—let him."

In my head, I could hear Sr. Benedicta, a fellow sacristan and a real jokester, crying out to a group of us rushing around before a service like a flock of headless birds: *Come on, people, work with me, work with me!* I bit my lip to keep from laughing at the thought. We then followed Sr. Hedwig across the street to the main house, where the Bishop gave us a blessing. We were officially on retreat.

After saying night prayers together and receiving communion, the six of us went upstairs to our rooms. My room was at the end of a long corridor, with only a tiny window for ventilation. The residents who normally occupied the house had covered the mirror in the hall bath with newspaper so we could not look at ourselves. The week was supposed to be about focusing on your soul, not your appearance. I lay down on the bed, not bothering to remove my garb. I knew I wouldn't fall asleep. The superior of the day possessed the only clock in the house, as we were forbidden clocks and watches. No one owned a cell phone back then.

At 3:00 a.m., the superior of the day rang the bell outside the chapel door. I stumbled from bed. We lined up in order and then processed downstairs for prayers. I then became the superior of the day and had charge of the dreaded clock. Once back upstairs, I couldn't sleep—except for the few moments before the damn clock went off at five minutes to six. To wake myself up, I pulled hard on the rope attached to the chapel bell. Our breakfast was one cup of coffee and one piece of toast—with either butter or jam, but not both—and one glass of water. Unfortunately, none of us had set up the coffee pot, an old electric percolator, before going to bed. Someone hastily got it going, and we stood gazing at it like Oliver Twist, clinging to our mugs, waiting for it to finish. As the person responsible for keeping us on track for the day, I poured the first cup before the coffee was fully perked and drank a weak dishwater version that still managed to burn a hole in my stomach.

We then read the morning office and performed culpa. For me, culpa was excruciating. You had to name aloud your faults against the holy rule as well as any personal sins or peccadillos you may have had. My childhood made the whole process of culpa a nightmare for me. I was raised to believe that if you were "bad" you brought shame on yourself and your entire family. My mother's infamous hiss of "Shame on you!" would accompany any deviation on my part from her version of correct behavior. So I had a difficult time acknowledging any benefit to culpa. I went first and rattled off the usual suspects—lack of humility, pride, disobedience, and speaking out of turn. After you gave your culpa, others were allowed to accuse you of faults you hadn't confessed. I paused and was met with silence. I sighed and sat back down. The process went on relatively well. Each person took his or her turn on the kneeler, listing the dregs of their souls until we came to the last man. His culpa was a digression into a Messiah complex. He went on at length about how everyone was out to get him and not truly accusing himself of any wrongdoing.

The group grew restless and cast furtive glances across the aisle. I was tired—no, exhausted—and I had a pounding headache. I was hungry, which was quickly erupting into my being "hangry." When the man finally ceased his diatribe, I stood up. I let him have it. I told him he had just made a mockery of culpa, that what he had just performed was *not* culpa and that he had the rest of the week to get his shit together. (Well, I didn't say shit, but I meant it.) I could hear the round of applause from the rest of the group in my head.

***

Shortly before eleven, Br. Ronald arrived to say mass. His key would not turn in the lock, and none of us moved to open the door. We'd been instructed not to open it under any circumstances. Br. Ronald was a large, arrogant man, and he glared at us for not coming to his aid. He vested and then looked at me. "You should have the altar set each day for mass, and you can clean up afterwards." I couldn't respond, but I knew I probably wasn't allowed to perform sacristan work during my retreat. I was secretly glad to do it, though, as it would help alleviate the boredom and restlessness I felt. I was compelled to work, to having some productive aspect to my life.

In the course of saying mass, Ronald prayed "for the soul of our departed sister, Gertrude." That's when we all learned that one of the founders of the Chapter had died. Sr. Gertrude was the first general counsel, the role of mediator between superiors and their classes when there were conflicts. I remembered her as a small, bird-like woman with bright eyes, who loved to straighten caps and veils and make sure everyone held their office books at equal height.

Sr. Hedwig arrived later that day to tell us that the viewing, Office of the Dead, and funeral mass would be held in the retreat house. "You are not to allow any of this to interfere with your retreat experience," she said with a pained look that obviously meant she knew it would and there wasn't a damn thing she could do about it. A few of the residents moved the set up for our retreat to the "fish bowl," the glass-walled chapel on the second floor, where only a few tiny side windows and a rickety old box fan provided ventilation. It was like being in an oven.

Downstairs, residents and sacristans worked to convert the first floor into a funeral home viewing room. The casket holding Sr. Gertrude arrived, and the funeral director opened it before the altar. The Bishop directed the setup. He ordered the placement of rugs, lamps, flowers chairs, tissues, fans and more. Sr. Gertrude's portrait hung on the wall next to the altar. A short time later, the photograph crashed to the floor. The Bishop ordered someone to pick it up, murmuring, "She's mad about something." We retreatants clustered on the stairs like children watching an adult party. That evening, the friends and family of Sr. Gertrude came to pay their respects. We stayed mostly upstairs and walked across the street to eat our meal in silence on the back patio of the main house.

***

Tuesday evening, the Chapter gathered to sing the Office of the Dead for Sr. Gertrude. The family sat to one side as the professed and novitiate stood in two double lines to say the prayers for the dead. Sr. Hedwig segregated our group from the rest of the Chapter, and afterwards we performed the ritual handwashing and reading of Psalm 91 upstairs in the fish bowl. My fellow sacristans were buzzing about, getting everything ready for the funeral mass the following morning. Two of the other women retreatants and I crept down the stairs, hoping to get to the kitchen, where there was a pitcher of water in the refrigerator. We were allowed one glass of water at bedtime, which had to be finished by the following morning. We were dressed in shorts and T-shirts, ready for sleep in the stifling upstairs heat. Chapter members were staying with the body overnight, and we could hear them saying the vigil prayers for Sr. Gertrude.

Sr. Janet, one of the sacristans, met us at the bottom of the stairs. The three of us stood there, looking at her, she at us. "Do you want to join the vigil?" she asked doubtfully, taking in how we were dressed. We shook our heads. She mused for a moment. Eva, one of the other women, made a motion of picking up a glass and drinking it down. We all looked at Janet like expectant dogs. "You want to go to the kitchen?" she asked. We nodded. She smiled. "Wait here." We sat down like those same obedient dogs on the steps. After evidently consulting with someone in authority, Sr. Janet returned. "OK, follow me and be quiet." The last injunction struck me as hilarious. We weren't supposed to talk. I guess we were capable of raising a ruckus otherwise. She led us behind the altar and the open casket and into the kitchen. We filled our water glasses with the cold refrigerated water, and then headed single file back to the steps.

***

For the funeral mass, we were seated as a group in front. The Bishop spoke in his eulogy of how blessed we were to have Sr. Gertrude die while on our retreat and how she was now in heaven, praying for us. Later that day, as we were all once again in street clothes, Sr. Hedwig came and told us we would be having our dinner in the youth house. The superior of the day pointed to her clothes and then held out her hands, shrugging her shoulders, as if to say "Like this?" Sr. Hedwig nodded. "You're fine, come on." We trooped over next door. There in the front room, tables had been set up and a group of formally dressed men and women were eating. They all stopped and stared when the six of us walked in. They were Sr. Gertrude's family, eating the wake dinner the Church had provided. Sr. Hedwig seated us at a table near the back. I felt foolish and out of place, like we were a troop of homeless people descending on a formal state dinner. The good news was the food was definitely a step up from the bland fare we had been eating, and there was even cake for desert.

The phone rang, and one of the sisters who had been serving the food answered. "No, not tonight. Sealing is at 7:00 p.m. tomorrow." The six of us looked at one another. We would find out that the Bishop canceled Chapter for that Wednesday because of the funeral. Wednesday was always the night of the sealing service for the seven-day retreatants. Each of the retreatants would kneel before the Bishop and be anointed with holy oil to "seal" their retreat experience. Because of the funeral, he made the decision to move it to Thursday.

I was already at a breaking point. I found myself looking from the fish bowl down to the street below at my parked car. I wanted to jump into it and drive home. I knew now I would never have made it in a traditional convent, with the constant rules and the monotony of the days. I had only experienced four days of enclosure and I was done. I wanted to read what I wanted to read, not just the office book or the bible. I wanted to eat good food. I was tired of the mushy, overcooked stuff we ate daily. I wanted my air-conditioned room at home. I wanted to be able to talk to someone, someone who would answer me verbally, a real conversation, not the one-sided stream I was experiencing of all of us praying to a god who kept his lips zipped. Most of the time, I was queasy and tired from lack of sleep, the food, and the unrelenting heat. To keep myself somewhat sane, I wrote in a notebook a series of rants about how much I wanted to get out of there. Sr. Hedwig had told us the door was open if we chose to leave. She didn't count on the cage of guilt and shame that kept me from running out.

***

Finally, Thursday night arrived. I thought, or hoped really, that the sealing would end the struggle, that it would make the next day and half easier. The choir sang as we took our seats up front, the rest of the Chapter watching us. The Bishop preached on our retreat experience, how we were once again being separated unto god. Then one by one, we went to the kneeler before him, and the Bishop anointed us with chrism oil. I sat back down in my seat, feeling empty and drained, wiped out by the tension of the week. I realized how my own anxiety and fears became the energy field that had kept me moving, a vortex that propelled me and drained me at the same time. I wanted to let that all go. The big miracle I was hoping for, the total acceptance of being in Chapter, of becoming the Bride of Christ, didn't happen. My chest tightened and a few tears slipped down my face. All I could see was failure—and of course, I blamed myself.

When the service ended, we returned to the retreat house. My fellow retreatants sat in the fish bowl, windows wide open, fan roaring, singing at the top of their lungs. They had evidently received a joy buzz from the sealing that I hadn't. I sat apart from the rest, some of whom were crying, some in a beatific daze. I was still the outsider, the one who didn't get it. God had not lifted me into a state of ecstasy. It was more proof to me I didn't belong here. I eventually drifted off to bed, leaving them to continue to annoy the non-church neighbors.

On Friday, we spent the day cleaning the entire house, stripping and remaking beds with fresh linens, doing laundry, cleaning bathrooms, washing down the kitchen, mopping floors, and vacuuming. It kept me occupied, but somehow made me even more antsy and anxious to leave. I remember writing how much I wanted this to be over, how the day would never end. I sensed the restlessness in the others as well, some unable to sit perfectly still during the daily prayers, legs shaking or feet tapping.

***

I was once again superior of the day on Saturday morning, the day the retreat was over. I rang the chapel bell with extra vigor, like bells ringing after a war is declared over. After mass, Br. Ronald gave us our final blessings, and we were done.

"Who is winning the NHL playoffs?" I asked. All of us were seated outside eating lunch. The Pittsburgh Penguins were vying for the

Stanley cup, and I hoped that they'd either won or were still in the running.

"One more game tonight, game seven. Hopefully the Pens will take them," Br. Ronald told me. I was thrilled.

Sr. Hedwig looked at all of us with a worried expression. It may have been my question or the haste of the out-of-town retreatants to leave that had her muse, "We hope that the funeral didn't ruin your retreat experience." No one replied. She pushed on. "Most brothers and sisters that come off retreat express the wish that the retreat never end." I shuddered with horror at that claim and wisely kept my mouth shut.

"We don't think it *ruined* anything, Sr. Hedwig. We are just eager to get home and share our beautiful experience with everyone," one of the out-of-towners said, as if in an effort to soothe Sr. Hedwig. I got the impression from Sr. Hedwig's tight-lipped smile that she wasn't buying that excuse.

***

My parents didn't ask anything about my being away. When I asked how things had been at home, my mother shrugged. "We're still here." I knew that she would be angry with me for at least a few days because I had failed in my duty to be her companion in the loneliness that was my parents' marriage. My father would rely on my mother for any information about what had happened to me while I was gone. We settled in to watch the hockey game, and the Pens won. It was as if I had never been away. It was just another Saturday night, me on the couch, my parents in their respective easy chairs, the television blaring, and cookies or cake or pie for a snack.

Retreat was one more hurdle accomplished, one more experience on the way to profession. Had I learned anything from being silent for a week? I had learned I could do it. I could go without saying one word to anyone for seven days and live to tell the tale. But my natural reticence had helped there. I had learned that I was uncomfortable without a list of tasks and jobs to complete, that my inner "girl with the clip board" was relentless, and that my self-worth was tied to what I could produce, perform, and give. I learned that I still would prefer to scrub a floor with a toothbrush than list my faults, because perfection trumps peace of mind and heart every time. I learned I loved my comfortable life and that poverty sucks. What I had not learned was to listen to the voice in my soul that said, *This life is not for you.*

Profession

I don't really recall pretending to be the blushing bride when I was growing up. I was never the little girl casting her Barbie's wedding day with my stuffed animals as the bridesmaids and ushers. All that attention focused on me, even for just a day, would have probably made me ill. My introverted self would have run to the nearest bathroom and bolted the door shut. And no wedding I've ever attended, no matter how lavish or small, was preceded by the funeral of the bride—that is, until I made my professed vows and married god.

Profession marked the change between the engagement phase of the relationship with Christ in the novitiate to that of the Bride relationship of the professed. We were telling god that we were signing up for a ten-year stint, at which point we could renew our professed vows or leave the Chapter with honor. Taking the professed vows and leaving before the term ended was akin to divorce—and in this case, the Bride always initiated the divorce, never the Groom. He would always be faithful, whereas the Brides were the ones who could become faithless.

The profession services spanned a three-day weekend. Friday evening was our "death." We buried all of our faults, sins, doubts, whatever made us less in god's eyes, so that on Sunday all god would see was his son reflected in the pure mirror of our souls and be pleased. My classmates and I sat in the front pews of St. Xavier's Chapel, waiting for the service to begin. It was a warm, humid spring night in early May of 1992. A simple pine casket draped in black stood at the back of the tiny church. We were to stand in front of it and recount aloud what made up our worst selves, everything that was wrong with us, effectively tossing it into the casket. We were encouraged to make a list of all that we wanted to bury. I watched as my fellow classmates furiously scribbled their last-minute faults. I stared at my own sliver of paper. It was short but loaded with self-loathing. I looked up at the crucifix on the wall behind the altar and wondered if this was what he wanted. Should we really dump our hidden underbelly of darkness? Maybe we should try to work with it, reclaim our shadows, and see that the dark and the light need to go together.

Sr. Hedwig, our novice mistress, had stood in front of us a few weeks before profession. "What you put in that casket should stay in that casket. Don't go looking for a shovel to unbury it. And don't allow anyone else to dig it up for you. People, particularly your closest family and friends, will remind you of your faults. Stop them. Say, 'I buried that at my profession and gave it to the Lord. It's finished and I am not going back.'" I watched her, a tiny bird-like woman, her hands wheeling and gesturing, animated in her belief that this was the truth she was proclaiming to all of us.

Sitting in the chapel that night, all I could feel was anger—anger that I wasn't good enough as I was, that none of us were, and that only by becoming something else could we please God. What I didn't understand at that time was how deeply sunk into depression I was, and my feelings of anger were a symptom of that depression. I longed for acceptance from god, from those around me; I couldn't accept myself as I was.

The choir began to sing, and one by one, my classmates went back to the doorway to place their faults in the casket. A thunderstorm whipped up, lightning crashing and thunder pealing. Some of the professed at the service made jokes later that old Scratch must have been in a rage over the lot of us turning from him and going with god. Or, I thought, maybe god isn't that happy with all of us. Maybe the storm is a warning: *Stop and think what you are doing.*

When it came time for me to go back to the casket, I saw my maid of honor, Tracy, standing at the opposite end of it, her back to the open door, holding my lit Paschal candle. She was a silent witness to my "death." Part of her position as my maid of honor was to remind me of when I was not in alignment with my vows, that I had indeed buried my faults this stormy night. I stood facing the rain-soaked doorway and calmly read my list, which was short but painful, the words written in red ink, like blood. I proclaimed my greed, envy, gluttony, anger. The underpinning of all of these sins was fear—fear of being seen, of being ignored, of being unloved, and of being unable to live up to the expectations of others. But did those demons truly leave me and willingly enter the casket that night? I know now and knew then the answer was no. The demons I carry inside are a part of me. My attempt to bury them probably sent them all into fits of laughing.

Bury us? You might as well throw yourself in there, love!

Denial and cover up would only allow these parts of myself time to seek ways to spill out into my life. All of the fuel in these demons was to be ignored and unused. The problem is that if the fuel is not used it can build into an inferno that will burn your life down.

I had heard some of the others wailing and crying over the storm's wrath, but I was calm, that soul-numbing calm that comes over you when you are just tired of trying. I blew out my candle with such force that the superior who was standing at the end of the casket jumped back in fright. With that short huff, I blew out *my* light, extinguishing my spiritual existence for now, until I would light my candle again on Sunday when I took my professed vows. I sat back down, looking out the side door at the slashing rain. I longed to walk out into that storm. After the service was over, I left to drive home. It seemed strange to be leaving without asking permission, without staying to clean up the church. The rain had ended and the night air was cool. I felt empty, hollow, disassociated. I wondered if this is what it felt like to be dead.

***

The next day was our "funeral." For the mass, the priests and the Bishop wore black vestments, and deaconates rolled in the black pall-covered casket. The congregation and the celebrants prayed for us as if we were dead. I sat watching the whole affair, knowing that I wasn't in that casket. I was in my seat with all the parts of me, good, bad, and indifferent. My classmates cheered and waved goodbye to the casket as the deaconates pushed it out of the church. Those who handled the empty casket made more jokes, about how heavy it was and how we must have been exceptional sinners. I had a headache right between my eyes, like a spike driving into my head. I asked to be excused from the lunch and went home.

    I was up for most of the night, unable to turn my mind off. Sunday's service was the culmination of five years of struggling. I wanted to call the whole thing off, but like many unsure brides, I was afraid—afraid of looking like a fool, of being embarrassed, of not being like the others who seemed to believe in what they were doing. Pride and perfectionism reared their twin ugly heads again. I tried to reason with myself. What's ten years? One decade of my hopefully very long life. Supposedly, I was already dead. I would be receiving a "do-over" tomorrow. Or a ten-year stretch, depending on how you wanted to look at it. I had been taught that the Bridegroom would never turn away anyone who wished to be his Bride. He should be more selective, I thought. What was I hoping to gain from this? My former desire to ensure my family's salvation had dried up over the past five years. A god who would wholesale condemn people to eternal pain didn't match up with the idea of the big JC who loved everyone no matter what. I knew I was simply lying down in the uncomfortable bed that I had made for myself.

***

    On Sunday morning, I got up early to head to the Mother House for mass. I managed for once to leave without seeing my mother, which was a mixed blessing. I had been relieved of yet another pointed questioning session, but I had guilt over not saying goodbye on this of all mornings. It felt like I was eloping, running off with someone my parents did not approve of. Add in the twist that I was an adult and capable of making my own decisions and my mind was even more chaotic and divided against itself.

    Heading over the bridge on my way to the Mother House, I wondered what it would be like to drive off it. The momentary thought of suicide pulled me up short. I managed to keep driving, my heart pounding in my ears. My stomach churned, and I was certain I would vomit. I paused after parking the car to pull myself together and squelch my rising panic. I fixed my scrabbling mind on minutia, walking slowly and deliberately, keeping my eyes fixed ahead. In the upstairs chapel of the main house, I knelt before the tabernacle. Did I pray? If wordless, formless chaotic emotions are prayers, then yes, I did pray. I clasped my office book with the happy death cross affixed to it against my heart. I heard no words of reassurance. The dread did not lift. I made my way downstairs to the Bishop's house and took my place with the others. I glanced around me. I wondered if any of them felt the same panic or if they were ready to take this step without reservation. Once again, I was the outsider, unable to fully be a part of what was happening around me.

After the mass and lunch, each of us dressed in our new white garb. Then, as in our aspirant step, the superiors dressed us with our veils and skullcaps. The long brown professed veil skimmed my shoulders, and a wooden crucifix hung from a brown cord around my neck. Holding my Paschal candle, I walked down the center aisle. I handed my candle to Tracy and lay down on the floor. The sacristans covered me with a gold pall. I buried my face in my arms, shuddering as if cold on the warm spring day. Over and over I repeated the words in my mind, *Help me. Help me. Help me.* Whom was I asking for help? Was I expecting an answer? Once again, I was laying down my life, the life I had been willing to throw away just a few short hours before.

A hand touched my shoulder. One of the deaconates helped me rise up from the floor. I took the few short steps to the kneeler, where I read the wedding vows, which ended with the words, "now and for all eternity." I would always be the Bride of Christ, even if I left, even if I ran from the room right at that moment. The Bridegroom was always faithful, even if the Bride was not. A priest lifted the back of my veil and cut a single snip of hair from my head, symbolizing the release of my strength, just as Sampson had lost his in the Old Testament. Christ would now be my strength. One of the priests held a crown of thorns over my head, saying, "Be crowned in the sufferings of this life that you may inherit the Brideship." Another of the priests slipped a plain gold band on the ring finger of my right hand. I was helped up and taken to kneel on a pillow before the Bishop. Another pall encircled me. The Bishop offered me a pyx with the gleaming white host inside. I leaned forward and pressed my lips to the glass, sealing the marriage with a kiss. I felt myself sinking, unable to keep up the charade I had carried on until that moment. I had no more strength. Unseen hands lifted me up and carried me from the room to the porch outside. I sat and wept.

***

If I could time travel, I would go back to that moment, to that scared and scarred weeping woman and put my arms around her. I would tell her that life would get better. I would tell her that the choices she had made to that point would have far-reaching consequences, and that not all of those consequences were bad. I would wipe away her tears and cradle her gently. I would tell her that I love her and that she would be OK because life is not just this moment, this accident, this mistake, this knowing. Life moves, changes, blurs, and refocuses itself in ways we can't understand while it is unfolding around us.

Somehow, I found the strength to get up from the chair, to walk to the car, and to go the celebration dinner. I accepted the congratulations of my brothers and sisters. I gave blessings to those who asked for them, and I continued to behave as if everything was fine.

Afterwards, I drove home and took off the long veil and the wooden crucifix. I squared my shoulders before going inside. Something had broken in me, and yet something had been shored up within me. I was like a broken limb, splinted until the bone grows back together.

After most weddings, the newlyweds head off on a romantic honeymoon to spend time alone. Profession was supposed to deliver a similar honeymoon phase, an afterglow that surrounded the new Brides of Christ. Any glow wore off for me as quickly as it came. I was already a wife, struggling to fulfill the marriage contract she had made. I was never a bride.

All True Vows

William the Martyr

I first met William at my Aspirant Investiture weekend. Sitting in the basement of St. Xavier's Chapel, I was adding to my prayer list. I felt rather than heard someone approaching. I looked up to see a man with strawberry blond hair, a ruddy face, and lean whittled features. I had no idea who he was. He was dressed in the brown clergy shirt of a first deaconate. He handed me a tiny scrap of paper and said in a low voice, "Please consider taking this under the pall." I took the paper from him, and he turned and walked briskly over to one of my classmates and made the same request. I watched him approach every single one of the future aspirants and do the same thing.

Our aspirant mistress, Sr. Mary Bernard, told us to write down whatever we most desired on a sheet of paper, a request list that we would carry on Sunday when we made our vows. "You can take requests from other people," she explained, "but you can also refuse anyone without telling them why. And you must write the request in your handwriting on your sheet of paper." On Sunday, the day of the service, we carried the lists next to our hearts, so my plan was to place it in my bra. The reason for carrying these requests on your body as you kissed the pyx containing the sanctified host was to place them in the closest proximity to god himself that you could on this earth. Sr. Mary Bernard told us to keep the list and look back on it years later. "You'll see so many of these things were given to you by the Lord," she said, beaming.

I unfolded the scrap of paper William had handed me.

Two lines of crabbed scrawl were written on it: "A diamond ring for Sr. A.; back healing for Sr. A."

I was puzzled. Who was Sr. A. and why did this young man want nothing for himself, only things for her? I shrugged and noted the two requests on my prayer list. Later, I learned that Sr. A. was William's then girlfriend and soon-to-be wife, Agnes. I realized these simple requests came from a humble heart who truly loved her.

My next encounter with William was in his role as a kitchen roustabout. Placed in charge of preparing food for events like Profession and Investiture, he was often in the kitchen, red-faced, sweating, yelling orders, dishing out guff, and running the show. At one of these events, he was making decorative baskets from watermelons. When someone asked him, "Do you want me to ball your fruit?" he threw his hands up in mock horror. "Ball my fruit? Ball my fruit?" he yelled. Everyone laughed at the bawdy humor. Seemingly everywhere, William was in perpetual motion, the first to get to work and the last to leave.

Part of the rules of the Chapter required that you make a silent retreat twice a year. I signed up as a new aspirant and arranged to spend the day in silence. Meals were served in the main house kitchen. When it was dinnertime, I lined up behind everyone else. William appeared in the doorway of the kitchen and noticed my "silent retreat" badge that let everyone know I wasn't responding to conversation. "Hey," he said gruffly, but not unkindly. "We've got a silent retreater here. Show respect; let her go first." The crowd in front of me turned to look, and my face flushed. Everyone parted like the Red Sea, and I moved to the front of the line, took my food, and sat in a corner by myself to eat. I had no idea that those in silence were given preferential treatment, but William evidently didn't forget the rules.

I knew William to be a man of faith. I stood with him at the altar at St. Xavier's as he conducted a communion service when Thomas was out of town on vacation. He addressed the prayers to the ciborium of hosts as if they were truly a living being—one who could hear and answer him, who understood that he was weak and mortal and yet loved him anyway. The sermon William preached that Sunday was one of the few I still remember. He talked about how god could intervene for anyone, anytime, if we only asked and trusted that god had our best interests at heart. His face flushed with his excitement as he described being hurt on the job. The insurance company first had denied him benefits, but god had intervened, and he received even more in benefits then he'd originally expected.

For years, the Mother House had no central large building for services. In the mid 1990s, the CRC decided to purchase an abandoned synagogue, just a street over from the main house, and convert it into a church, calling it the Temple of the Risen Christ. It would be the first building dedicated solely to worship services at the Mother House and would be large enough to hold the big gatherings for Easter, Investiture, and Profession. Work began inside and out to renovate the place and convert it into a church.

The bulk of the heavy construction fell on a few of the men with experience in the building trades. William was one of these men since he worked for a company that constructed new homes. On a Friday in late spring, William was working on the Temple roof without a safety harness when he fell to his death. The workers placed a call to the Bishop as well as to the local paramedics. The Bishop later said he saw William's spirit dancing and moving around the crushed skeleton it had once inhabited, ignoring the Bishop's pleas to return and come back to life. The paramedics could do nothing for William, and he was pronounced dead at the scene.

Bad news travels far more quickly than good, but I heard nothing about the tragedy until the next day when I was working at the Mother House. I was in the chapel of the main house when Thomas; his brother, Jerome; Jerome's wife, Elizabeth; and William's wife, Agnes, came into the room. Thomas ordered me to light the altar candles. He opened the tabernacle and gave communion to Agnes, who knelt on the floor with Jerome and Elizabeth on either side of her. Agnes looked wrung out, almost limp, her face white and drawn save for the dark circles under her eyes.

Thomas would later tell me that he would have never given Agnes communion if she had shown any anger at god for taking her husband. I didn't respond to him, but inwardly his thinking revolted me. If William were my husband, my anger at him, at the church, and yes, at god, would know no bounds. Thomas was saying that god would not permit Agnes to question why this had happened. Why was William up on that roof that day, a day he was supposed to be off work? Why wasn't he wearing a safety harness? And if Thomas's god was not big enough to take the anger of one distraught and anguished woman, what a pathetic excuse for a god was he worshipping?

The CRC held the funeral in the mission house, a tearful Agnes sitting by the coffin. People murmured that her true Bridegroom would be there to comfort her. But a spirit can't take the place of William's warm presence in bed with her, I thought. As the funeral cortege passed the still-under-construction temple, a group of workers held up a sign with a quote from Joshua 24:15: "As for me and my house, we will serve the Lord."

The temple renovations continued, and now the CRC had its very own martyr. The Bishop raised William's death to the status of legend, and he repeatedly told us of how god would use this tragedy to bring souls to the kingdom, how it would inspire young people to be on fire for Christ. I wondered how much of this story was to assuage the Bishop's own guilt regarding what had happened to William.

The first time I walked into the newly renovated building, I saw on the wall above the interior doorway an enlarged portrait of William on his wedding day. A plaque stated that he'd given his life for the construction of this house of god. I felt sick. The photo showed a young man in the prime of his life, his face turned towards his new bride.

I came to see Agnes as another Lot's wife, who had been turned into a pillar of salt—unable to move forward, held fast in time by an event beyond her control, and then controlled by those who wanted her to behave a certain way, a model of sanctity and submission. I was sad for Agnes and angry with those who treated her this way. The whole awful episode peeled away another layer of the veneer around the church for me.

All True Vows

Professed Day of Retreat

As a young child, I remember attending my great aunt Rena and great uncle Victor's fiftieth wedding anniversary celebration. Rena wore a silver-colored gown, all sparkling and shiny, with an enormous corsage on her shoulder. Victor, a dairy farmer, who normally wore overalls and a flannel shirt, looked very uncomfortable in his new dark suit and tie. When they danced together alone, however, you could see the love that had lasted between them for fifty years.

My first anniversary as a professed Bride of Christ was a bit different. On a frigid morning in February 1993, I struggled to lift the heavy hood of my first car, a Chevy Nova. It was about twenty degrees outside, with a wind chill in the single digits. I had parked my car behind the house, and it was buried in a layer of snow and ice. The car was a fuel injector model; it had a carburetor that simply refused to work in the cold. After rising at five, dressing in my white garb and then adding warm layers, I was bundled up like an Eskimo. I sprayed the choke valve in the carburetor with starter fluid and cursed my stupidity, tears freezing on my cheeks. I should have insisted on taking the one garage spot, swapping my car with my father's. Finally, the engine whined to life, and I scraped the windshield. I shivered in the car, not daring to turn on the heater. All I would receive in return was a blast of frigid air. I parked in front of one of the abandoned houses near the Mother House and slipped off my hat to tug on my veil.

The first-floor hall of the Mother House was filling up with the warm, sleepy bodies of the professed brothers and sisters. I took my seat in the back and leaned my head against the wall. All around me, people were dozing. One poor man even snored occasionally and snapped his head back in embarrassment. The familiar smells of strong disinfectant, faulty plumbing lines, carpet dust, and human funk filled the air. At six, we said the morning office together. Tired hollow voices rose and fell in the chanting of the words. We then sat down and waited for the Bishop to arrive. I dozed, awakened only by the sound of water pipes clanking and banging overhead. One of the residents was clearly violating the ten-minutes-only shower rule, making it impossible for us seated in the back to hear the sermon.

Sr. Felicity, the assistant mother general, finally dismissed us to go with our individual classes and meet for culpa. My stomach churned, empty and troubled. I hated this even more than the early rising. As far back as kindergarten, my report card noted I was unable or unwilling to take criticism. I had learned early on that perfection was safety; if everything was "just so," as my mother put it, then no harm could come to you. If someone told me there was something wrong with me, it threw me into a panic, and my response was to lash back with anger. Now I was in a position where I could not respond if my fellow classmates accused me of anything. The little girl I had been still lived inside me, desperate to be perfect and thus safe.

My class was the last to be professed and so we drew the short straw; our group met in one of the basements, a room normally used as a preschool. Toys and books lined the walls. On the floor, a pillow draped with a chasuble and crucifix, flanked by two candles in votive cups, served as our altar. Another pillow served as the kneeler. We trooped in, taking our places on the cold metal folding chairs arranged before the altar setup. As Chapter order was reversed that day, the youngest person among us went first.

I don't remember what was said that morning or who accused whom of what. It's all a blur to me now. I just remember I was grateful when it was over. I took down the setup for the "chapel" and then went out into the cold morning light with the others. We snagged coffee from the main house, and I drank it greedily, desperate for the caffeine and sugar fix. The smokers among us lit up. Other classes who had finished early joined our group; comments on how quickly we were finished earned laughs, while remarks on the length of some of the groups' culpas brought headshakes and groans.

No one was allowed into any area where a class was still holding culpa. Finally, we were permitted back into the first floor of the main house. We were supposed to remain in silence, but that went out the window. The day now had the atmosphere of a reunion, with people who lived out of town or who never came to Chapter, save this one day (for a variety of reasons), catching up with one another.

Finally, Sr. Felicity called us to order and we took our places again. Mass began, and as each of us went to receive communion, we first knelt before the Bishop who blessed our professed rings and if he was led, gave us a word from the Lord. I still clung to the hope that what the Bishop spoke in these moments were the words of Christ to me personally, not just some well-meaning platitude the man had come up with on his own. That day he leaned toward me and said, "In your quiet and reserve, you bring me great comfort." Were these the Bishop's words or was he truly speaking for god? All of my life I had struggled with being an introvert, knowing the world placed far more emphasis on those who were outgoing. Was god himself telling me that he was ok with me, just as I was?

The novitiate was required to serve and clean up the luncheon that followed mass. But there was still plenty of work for the sacristans to do, and I joined with the others to clean up and check the house chapels. I had nine more years in front of me as a professed. As is often the case, not knowing the future can truly be a blessing.

Sharon Downey

Thyroid Cancer — 1993

I was one of those lucky people who, until I was in my thirties, had managed to avoid the healthcare system. I never broke any bones, tore any ligaments, or needed stitches. I had the usual childhood diseases, but I never spent a day in a hospital. I never received anesthesia or had an operation.

It was 1993, I was 32, and my lucky streak was about to end. One Wednesday night after Chapter, I was talking to Grace. In the midst of our conversation, she reached her hand to my veil and brushed it back, peering at my neck. "What are you doing?" I asked.

"Come on, we need a mirror," she replied, leading the way up the stairs to the powder room across from the chapel. Grace positioned me in front of the vanity. "Swallow," she commanded me. I complied and saw for the first time a pea-sized lump move up and down alongside my Adam's apple. I stared at it, put my fingers on it trying to stop it, to make it hold still. My eyes locked with Grace's in the mirror.

"You didn't know it was there?" she asked.

I shook my head dumbly.

"I had one, too," she explained. "That's how they knew about the thyroid cancer." The word cancer seemed to echo off the walls of the tiny room.

But I am healthy! How? Why? I thought.

Grace put her hands on my shoulders, her voice gentle. "You need to have that looked at. You should go to my doctor. He's very good, very thorough." She wrote his name down for me and then gave me a warm hug. "Don't be afraid," she said with a smile. "He'll be able to help you." We left the bathroom and went into the chapel. "I'll pray for you," she whispered and gave me another hug.

***

Now the hard part came—telling my parents about the lump in my throat. I waited until the weekend to say anything, and naturally, I told my mother. I held a hand mirror up in front of me and showed her the tiny lump.

"Oh, that's nothing!" she exclaimed, much too loudly. "Just go to the doctor, you'll see. Everything will be fine."

Later, I heard her telling my father about it. "What if it's bad?" she asked him. I couldn't hear his response. I don't think at the time that I realized how scared they were for me.

I made an appointment to see Dr. Radfar, Grace's gruff, no-nonsense endocrinologist, and my parents came with me for my first visit. My father, naturally, said nothing except to ask if "this guy" was any good, and even my normally voluble mother was silent as we drove to the appointment. Dr. Radfar probed my neck, had me drink water while he watched my throat as I swallowed, and asked me endless questions. Was I tired? Did I feel excessively hot or cold? Did I have dry skin, cracked fingernails, digestive issues? Had I gained or lost weight? With each shake of my head and my small-voiced, "No," I could see his frustration building.

"The only way we will be able to know if the lump is of concern or not is for you to have a whole-body scan," he told me. "We'll also need some bloodwork."

We drove home in silence, all of the unanswered questions still swirling around us. I looked out the car window and kept touching the tiny lump, feeling it slowly move up and down in my neck. My mind went back to its usual routine of self-accusation and blame. Naturally, this had to be my fault. I had either done something or not done something I was supposed to do, and now I had a bizarre lump in my throat that may or may not be cancer. I fell back on my oldest ingested teachings from childhood. If bad happened to you, it was your own damn fault. If good happened to you, god was feeling generous.

My blood tests showed my thyroid levels were normal, which was why I had no symptoms. At the end of April, I went to Mercy Hospital for my whole-body scan. I lay on a flat and narrow gurney while a machine, inches from my face, slowly moved its way down my body to my midsection. The resulting pictures showed half my thyroid had ceased to function and that the nodule was cold, meaning I had a greater chance of the lump being malignant.

I spent hours reading about the thyroid, its functions, and the types of cancer that can develop there. I learned that most thyroid cancers could be completely cured. A few weeks after I'd had the scan, I returned to Dr. Radfar. He explained that the usual course of action would be to have a core needle biopsy. He would insert a hollow needle into the nodule, extract cells, and send them off to be analyzed. He cautioned me that the test was not foolproof. A false negative could be obtained if the needle would miss the cancer cells. I told him I wanted to think it over before making a decision on having the biopsy. I was and still am terrified of needles, and the thought of someone sticking me in the neck with one made me queasy.

Dr. Radfar recommended a head and neck surgeon, Dr. Arena, who had operated on Grace as well. I made an appointment to see the surgeon. I spoke to my superior, Sr. Louisa, about what was going on. "You should write to the Bishop and ask him what to do," she told me. "That way, he'll know to pray for you about this." I wrote the note and dropped it into his mailbox. The following week, I received a typewritten response. In it, the Bishop instructed me to take the approach of "wait and see," attend the next miracle service, which was scheduled for the end of June, and see what god would do. I should only consider surgery as a last resort.

I read over and over the Bishop's response to me. If I followed his instructions, another two months would go by. I fingered the lump in my throat, the hardness of it in the middle of the soft flesh of my neck making me feel ill. I needed to have this thing removed. I didn't want to wait. Each day I suffered from headaches and stomach pains from attempting to carry on as if nothing was wrong with me. I kept up the appearance of normalcy and calm, while inside my fear roiled under the surface. I was doing my usual I'm-OK-everything's-fine act, so that I could placate the fear and apprehension of those around me, particularly my parents. Denial was my drink of choice—but I wasn't sure how much more of it I could consume.

***

My appointment with Dr. Arena happened the second week of May. He walked into the exam room, a tall, imposing man with a deep voice and large, shapely hands. "I recommend that you have the nodule removed," he told me. "Once it is biopsied, we'll determine if it is malignant, and if so, then I would remove your entire thyroid. The biopsy will be performed while you are under anesthesia, so you won't have to have two operations. If you need follow-up treatment, Dr. Radfar would take care of that."

After examining my throat and asking me a few more questions, Dr. Arena sat down in front of me. "I need to inform you of the risks of this surgery." He pointed to a plastic model of the human head on the counter. The side was cut away so you could see the inside. The thyroid gland appeared as a butterfly-shaped blob. "One of the risks is that I could cut one of your vocal cords, in which case you would be hoarse for the rest of your life. If I cut both of your vocal cords, you would never speak above a whisper."

I sat perched on the edge of the chair, rigid, staring at him, my hand reflexively covering my throat. I'm sure my face must have shown my horror.

Dr. Arena bent closer, gently touched my other hand, and said, "But I've never done either of those things to any patient, and I don't intend to start with you."

I nodded dumbly. A voice, one that I had spent much of my life ignoring, dousing, and boxing up, came whispering into my mind. *You can trust this man*, it said.

"Would you like some time to think this over?" Dr. Arena asked. My head shook vehemently, tears prickling my eyes.

"I want this over with," I said, ever my mother's daughter. The nurse brought in the consent forms, and she placed me on Dr. Arena's surgical schedule. Before the surgery, Dr. Arena ordered another scan of my thyroid. In the short time between my first and second scans, the lump had grown in size. I was even more convinced I had made the right decision to go ahead with the surgery, but I was still terrified.

***

The weekend before my surgery offered me a diversion. Grace's daughter Marie was getting married. After the service, the Bishop called me over to him and gave me a blessing, stating he would pray for me. He did not comment on my ignoring his advice.

At mass the following morning, I stood at the altar with Thomas as he cleaned the chalice. There was usually wine left after the distribution of communion, and sometimes Thomas would offer me the cup to drink from before he would finish the wine and cleanse the vessel. As I usually had not eaten, I would take only a small sip, the wine burning my stomach. I handed him back the cup. As he cleansed it, he turned toward me and in a low voice said, "The Lord says to you, you will not die." I stood blinking at him, trying to hold back the tears. He dipped his hands in the dish, wiped them with the finger towel, and turned toward the lectionary to read the closing prayers. I picked up the dish and turned to enter the sacristy. A huge sob grabbed me in the chest and exploded out of my lips, loud enough for the entire, now-silent congregation to hear. I collapsed onto the step and wept like a banshee. Thomas chuckled and said to the group before him, "It's OK, she's alright. Everything's fine." I was embarrassed and worse yet, felt I was out of control. Was I afraid of dying? I hadn't given it much thought. I had locked the fear of death tight in the basement of my subconscious, but it had seen its opportunity to make a loud and rather dramatic appearance.

***

My surgery was scheduled for the following Friday. Lying in my hospital gown, I was questioned over and over about my medical history, and I had the distinct impression that most of my questioners were incredulous as to my having reached the age of thirty-two without ever having been operated on or hospitalized, for that matter. Rolled into the freezing operating room, I was still trying to be in control, talking to the nurses until the medication to knock me out took hold and plunged me into darkness.

I don't remember waking up in recovery. The drugs must have had a lingering amnesiac effect on me. Later, in my hospital room, my mother recounted what happened in the recovery area. "I leaned down close to you and told you that Dr. Arena said the nodule was cancer and that he had to remove your whole thyroid," she said, shaking her head. "The doctor said you were lucky. It was a big lump, and he was afraid it would have spread into your neck and chest." I lay on the bed, my throat sore, my head aching. "And you know what you said to that when I told you?" my mother went on, sitting forward in her chair and reaching to stroke my arm. I shook my head. "You had one great big tear roll down your face and you whispered to me, 'Now what?'" She smiled at me with pride on her face.

As ever, I was off to the next step, what was next on the to-do list. Topping the list were fighting cancer and making a complete recovery, both of which I went on to do. I had two treatments of radioactive I-131, which acts as a heat-seeking missile and is absorbed by any remaining thyroid tissue in the body, effectively killing it. I have a slight scar on my throat and must take a daily dose of replacement hormone to give my body what my thyroid provided.

***

What no one in the church hierarchy, including the Bishop, Thomas, or my superior, ever expressed was a curiosity about why this cancer had occurred or why it was located in my throat. When I returned to church, to my sacristan duties, no one commented on my surgery. Yet in time, one more person from St. Xavier's was diagnosed with thyroid cancer, making three women from the same congregation a sisterhood in this disease.

It wasn't until years after I left the church that I learned about the chakras, the seven energy centers of the body, and I began to understand the relevance of having cancer in my throat. The throat chakra is our voice, and it controls our ability to communicate. When Dr. Arena, told me about the risks of the surgery, he was telling me about the potential for me to be silenced. Had my fear of drawing attention to myself, of going along to get along, made me physically ill? My heart and soul tell me the answer is yes. It would take many more years before I found the courage to speak my own truth and to truly own it.

Baptism

When I was about twelve years old, my family drove the fifty miles from Pittsburgh to Moraine State Park for a picnic. At the center of the park was Lake Arthur, a calm sparkling jewel ringed with trees. After changing into our swimsuits, we laid our blankets on the grass. I walked out to the lake and waded into the water. Up to a point, I could walk along the sandy bottom. I couldn't swim, and so I was cautious as I moved farther out. What I didn't know was that there was a sudden drop off. Losing my footing, I floundered and went under. My parents were on the shore, and my brother, who had joined me in the water, had wandered off. There were no lifeguards. I struggled to pull myself upright. I managed to surface, but the waters closed over my head a second time. I panicked, thrashing and struggling. Someone, I never found out who, pulled me up by grabbing me around the shoulders. I sputtered and coughed, brushing off any more help from my rescuer. I dragged myself out of the water, stumbled across the grass, and dropped onto the blanket next to my parents, where I remained for the rest of our visit. I just sat there, looking at the calm lake, shivering in the bright sunlight—more from fear than from cold.

My fear of water came up years later, but in a very different context. I missed Chapter the Wednesday night that Russ Bixler showed up as the guest speaker. He was the founder of Cornerstone TV, channel 40, the local all-Christian programming station. I viewed Russ and his wife, Norma, as probably two of the most annoying individuals on the planet. They were smug, self-righteous, and self-satisfied. I knew they were coming, so I made up an excuse and stayed home. Guest speakers were a mixed bag, ranging from the interesting to the completely obnoxious. I included Russ and Norma with the latter.

Annie and I had grown to be close friends over the years. While some, like Grace, were more content to follow the party line and go along with whatever happened in the CRC, Annie saw things through more cynical, call-it-bullshit-if-it's-bullshit eyes. She called me the night after Russ and Norma's appearance. "You missed it," she started in at once. "The Bishop is pissed."

"Why? I thought he liked those fools."

"Not anymore. Russ called for people to come up and get the Holy Spirit, and a bunch of them did, some of the old timers too."

"What's wrong with that? Ain't we all supposed to be leaky vessels?"

"Well, according to the Bishop, none of us should have got up, 'cause we're all spirit-filled Christians. After he was done praying with everyone, Russ come up to the Bishop and told him, 'Well, a bunch of them got saved tonight!' rubbing it in his face."

I snorted. "Oh, for crying out loud, like two kids fussing on a playground—who's bigger and better?"

Annie continued, "Yeah, well the Bishop is having every superior call all of their class members. He wants to know where you were baptized and when you first got the Holy Spirit."

"Baptized? I was baptized when I was a baby!"

"Not good enough," she said. "Weren't you ever immersed?"

"No," I answered. "No one ever asked me if I was. In fact, no one ever said anything about it!"

"Well, they might make you do it," Annie replied.

I thought the whole thing was ridiculous. What difference did it make if someone dunked me under cold water or not?

My superior, Sr. Louisa, called me the next evening. True to Annie's word, she grilled me about my spiritual experiences. I told her what I had told Annie, innocently believing that nothing would come from telling her the truth. I couldn't have been more wrong. "You've never been immersed?" she asked, her voice taking on a somewhat hysterical pitch.

"No, no one ever said anything about doing that."

"Well, Jesus was immersed," she replied.

My automatic go-to response almost shot out of my mouth. *Yeah, the Roman government also nailed him to a cross—should I try that too?*

"You're going to have to be immersed," she told me.

I panicked. I still could not swim. I explained this to Louisa, relaying the story of my near drowning in Lake Arthur, confident this would elicit sympathy, but she wasn't budging. Having found out my unsatisfactory past, one of her own flock, she had to get me back on the straight and narrow. Since she was the Mother General's blood sister, there was even more urgency for this slip up to be rectified.

"Br. Patrick will take care of it," Louisa informed me.

"Where?" I practically whined the question. I could picture myself in a swimming pool in someone's backyard, while the neighbors next door, grilling hot dogs, got a spectacle to go with their cookout.

"There is a pool under the floor of the mission house. No one has used it for a while, but I'm sure he can take care of it. And I'll be there with you, so you won't be scared. It will be real quick. I promise." I thought the next words from her lips would be she would buy me a beer afterwards. But now I wasn't scared. I was angry. My years of complying with anything that the authorities had demanded wasn't enough—and all because one old man's knickers were in a twist.

***

I'm ashamed now to admit it, but I showed up at the appointed time with a change of dry clothes. I had to wear a musty-smelling white baptismal robe over my shorts and T-shirt. Br. Patrick, a bear of man who moved and spoke slowly, had already filled the pool, but the water was still chilly. He helped Louisa and me into the water and then climbed in after us. The water came up to around my hips, and I shivered from the cold. Patrick read that as a sign of fear.

"Rather than dip you backwards, I'm going to hold you by the elbows. You just bend your knees and lean forward till the water is over your head. I'll pull you right up."

I nodded. I looked over at Louisa. Her pursed lips told me she was upset she had to do this but felt it was her duty. All this, I thought, so that a check mark can go next to my name. I cursed to myself.

Patrick murmured the prayer, "I baptize you in the name of the Father, Son, and Holy Spirit."

I flexed my knees, screwed my eyes shut, took a deep breath, and plunged forward under the water, with Patrick pulling me up almost immediately. I sputtered and gasped and staggered on my feet, but Patrick caught me around the shoulders. He then clambered out of the pool and helped Louisa and me out of the water.

"See, that wasn't so bad," Louisa said in saccharine tone. I knew better than to respond to her, because my reply would not have been civil. I thanked Patrick and went into the first-floor bathroom to towel off and get dressed. That night on the drive home, with the warm summer air helping to dry my hair, I berated myself.

You should have lied, told them you were baptized at some camp when you were a kid. How the hell would they ever know you had been telling the truth or not?

Then my anger took a different tack.

You should have just told them you wouldn't do it, let them throw you out, see how long it took them to figure out they lost a good work horse.

The two streams of thought fought back and forth in my mind as I flew over the miles to home. I suddenly realized that neither of these points was the one that truly mattered. It came down to how much I was willing to put up with, to withstand, to endure in order to belong. That amount would shrink more and more in the time I had left before my professed vows were over.

All True Vows

Tracy

> *Words, in my not so humble opinion, are our most inexhaustible means of magic, capable of inflicting harm and remedying it.*

The above quote by Albus Dumbledore, the great wizard of JK Rowling's vivid imagination, is lacking one small twist, in my very humble opinion. To deny people our words, to refuse to communicate with them, and to turn our backs with no explanation why, can cause the greatest amount of harm. Not to engage, much like the shunning Amish communities do, or to break communion with the "sinner" creates a rift far deeper than any angry words can make. My shunning of Tracy is the biggest regret I have from my time within the Chapter.

I chose Tracy to be my maid of honor at my novice step. The maid of honor carries the Bride's Paschal candle, witnesses her taking a new name, and then helps to dress her in her new garb. She witnesses her burial at profession and her solemn marriage vow. The maid of honor is responsible to pray for the Bride and to help her keep her vows, to caution her when she is failing the Bridegroom. I chose Tracy because she attended St. Xavier's. We were all clannish that way, keeping to ourselves, and Thomas definitely encouraged that behavior.

I found myself fascinated by Tracy, and yet confused by her as well. She was beautiful, smart, funny, and charming. She embraced the vowed life, able to remember flawlessly to say "we," (meaning "the Lord and I") rather than "I," something I could never manage to do. Yet there was a darkness that seemed to surround her, a sadness, as if there were things in her past she was all too ready to bury and forget. Tracy threw herself into the children's ministry, and the kids loved her. I think she showered the children with the love and acceptance that she longed for from herself.

Four years into my professed life, Thomas's wife, Lena, having had enough of the control freak she had married, left him. Thomas, in his typical playing-to-the-balcony style, portrayed himself as the abandoned, cast-off husband, with no one to cook his meals or wash his socks.

More importantly, he was no longer having sex.

One Saturday, as I was struggling to put wet linens into the basement washer, I heard Thomas calling my name. My long-standing tactic of ignoring him didn't work. "Come up here!" he bellowed.

Sighing, I climbed the steps.

"What?" I asked, no preliminary pleasantries clouding my obvious displeasure. He went into a rant about how he'd been abandoned, first by his wife, and then by his congregation, who had left him to fend for himself.

"What did you do before you were married?" I asked.

He left my valid question unanswered and went on a diatribe about how great his sex life had been with Lena and how he was capable of bringing her to multiple orgasms. I don't know what turned my stomach more—the words he spoke or his own inability to see me as a full human being, not some dumping zone for his frustrations. I turned, reached for the doorknob to the cellar stairs, and left him without responding. He had no awareness of the utter inappropriateness of his comments.

Thomas then turned to Tracy, first for sympathy, later for romance. Soon, they were a couple—despite the fact that Thomas was still married, still a priest, and still Tracy's pastor. The news of their relationship spread like wildfire within the Mother House. Tracy called me at work, revealing the passionate kiss that Thomas had given her after their meeting in a bar somewhere. "This is just so right," she said repeatedly, as if trying to convince herself that it was. I hung up the phone, sickened by what I had heard. By the following Wednesday after they had begun dating, I had to face them both. Tracy was over the moon, and Thomas was behaving like a lovesick Romeo, devouring Tracy with his eyes.

Tracy called me at work the next day. When I saw her work number come up on my phone, I flinched. I sat there, watching the light flash, hearing the phone ring until it clicked over to voicemail. The message she left me was long and rambling, delivered in a breathy tone of satisfaction and longing. She told me about how much Thomas loved her, how she knew from their very first kiss that their relationship was meant to be. My stomach clenched, yet I was unable to put down the phone. It was like listening to a train wreck.

Thomas had managed to completely charm and dazzle Tracy. He knew exactly which buttons to push to make her want to be with him, to convince her the relationship was god's will. I knew what Tracy wanted from me—a confidant, a cheerleader for a relationship whom everyone else was condemning as wrong and sinful. I knew that I truly didn't care about the sinful part; they were both adults and Lena no longer wanted Thomas. What bothered me was Thomas's manipulation tactics and that Tracy was so blind to them. The situation revolted me. I know now I was seeing in her behavior my own naivety and willingness to suspend belief about Chapter life. Her behavior was a mirror for my own—and I didn't like what I saw.

So how did I respond? Did I call Tracy back, tell her point blank that I thought she had lost her mind, and condemn her for her gullibility? Did I try to reason with her, make her see that Thomas was playing her for a fool? Did I ask her what she hoped to gain from this relationship—if she really believed that Thomas was the soulmate she claimed he was? Was I honest, open, and willing to expose myself to her anger? No. I was a coward. I ducked Tracy's phone calls, her increasingly pleading, tear-filled messages asking me for my support and friendship. I refused to meet the challenge of her anger and disappointment over my lack of support. I froze her out of my life. I treated her as if she were under an evil spell, and I incorrectly assumed that I was powerless to help her break it. I didn't even try. When I next saw Tracy at the Mother House, I shunned her. I turned away from her and did not speak to her. For her part, Tracy simply followed my lead, not speaking to me as well.

We passed the remaining years of my time in Chapter in silence, neither of us acknowledging the other. Thomas eventually left the church. The relationship between him and Tracy ended, but the silence between Tracy and me went on. No one ever questioned the strange behavior between the two of us; no one ever accused me of it in culpa. It was as if no one else could see how we treated one another, or maybe they didn't care.

Looking back, I bitterly regret what I did to Tracy. I punished her for Thomas's avaricious lust and for someone he could control. She was a plaything for him, something to amuse him for a time. If I could redress one thing from my years in the Church, it would be to tell Tracy how truly sorry I am for all of the pain I caused her.

All True Vows

The Nightmares and My Meeting with the Bishop

The wine spills from the cup, slowly, slowly, in time-lapse mode, drop by drop. Red pearlescent liquid sprays the carpet, the kneeler, my white vestment. I scramble, lurch, and twist my body to catch the cup, its bright metal reflecting the sunlight. It arcs to the floor in a graceful dance, propelled by gravity and the timeless motion of the universe. My lips stretch open in a grimace of shock and dismay. I can do nothing to stop this from happening, and yet I must. I am the guardian of the cup and what it contains, holy and blessed wine, transubstantiated into blood that cleanses every fault and failing. My hands were anointed years ago by the holy chrism, bound together with the cincture's cord, and given in service to the divinity here in this chalice. And in this moment, this horrible moment, I am failing. I am incapable of stemming the tide, the tide of blood that pours from the vessel onto the floor, down the aisle, down the stairs, washing everything, staining everything. So much blood. All the while, he stands beside me, laughing, his hands spread wide, the cup gone from his fingers—dressed in his priestly robes, bedecked in satin and linen, glorious in a golden chasuble, a peacock preening and displaying his magnificence. He throws his head back and laughs at my horror, my disgrace, my shame, yet he openly flaunts his shame, his disgrace, his fall from righteousness. Over and over the cup spills, the blood falls, and he continues to laugh, to take delight, to revel in the dissolution of trust and belief that blackens him.

My subconscious, my true or Higher Self, had learned early on that the only way to communicate with me effectively was through my dreams. My fearful ego was able to shut down most of its messages during my waking hours. Sleep allowed my Higher Self a platform to get my attention, forcing me to look at things my ego was choosing to block out. Since Thomas's marriage had blown up and he had latched on to Tracy, I had begun having nightmares. Like a tape loop, they resurfaced night after night from my subconscious. They were all set at St. Xavier's, and I was serving at the altar. In the dreams, Thomas would drop the chalice, wine spilling everywhere, or I would fall down the steps, clutching the chalice while Thomas laughed. The dreams kept coming, all in the same vein. My role in these nightly bruisings from the subconscious was that I was responsible, I was the adult who was supposed to stop this terrible event from happening. Trouble was, I couldn't stop anything. The feeling of being out of control was something I had never learned to handle. I was exhausted, and I couldn't see a way to stop the dreams.

I needed to confide in someone, to get another perspective. I wrote the Bishop a letter describing the dreams, noting their repetitive nature and the fact that they essentially destroyed my sleep. Every night my subconscious was offering up the same bill of fare, and I wanted it to stop. I reasoned that since Thomas was under the direct authority of the Bishop, the Bishop had an obligation to do something about his behavior. I wouldn't have cared if the Bishop told me I needed an exorcism; I would have said sign me up. I put the note in the mail slot and went back to more sleepless nights.

My superior handed me the response from the Bishop the following Wednesday. It was the equivalent of being told to report to the principal's office. On the lower right-hand corner he wrote, "JMJ, See me Wed night." I stared at it, a crawling, squeamish sensation rumbling in my gut.

My superior was no help. "Don't worry. Just go see Johnny, and he will take you to the Bishop's office."

Sure. Great. Simple. No problem. Why couldn't he just tell me to wrap myself in about a dozen scapulars, drink a bottle of holy water, or say a few rosaries while massaging my scalp?

Holding the note in my hand, I found Johnny. "Oh yeah, you're on the schedule. Follow me." I trooped after him up the steps and across the hallway into the Bishop's house. I nervously looked around, having never been in this inner sanctum before. Johnny led me into a sitting room and pointed to a velvet-covered chair. I sat down, the seat crackling under me, the springs sinking toward the floor.

I looked up at Johnny, my eyes wide in sheer horror. "Oh my god, I broke it," I whispered.

He chuckled. "You, you little thing? No, my big behind did a number on that chair a long time ago. The Bishop will be in soon." I clutched my hands in my lap and tried not to think about throwing up.

I heard a toilet flush and then the Bishop's humming. As he walked in, I struggled to rise from my seat. "No, no, sit down, sit down." He waved his hand and lowered himself into a chair across from me. "Now, what can I do for you?" he asked quietly.

I burst into tears and put my head into my hands. I had no idea where this sudden storm burst had come from, and I was both scared and embarrassed.

"I…I don't know." I wiped my face. "I don't know what to do."

The Bishop looked at me and slowly shook his head. He evidently was used to people in his office having meltdowns. "I don't know either." He rubbed his hands over his knees. He smelled of aftershave. He'd slicked back his hair with water, just like my father. "I don't know what to do with him, Mary Joseph. I asked him to go on a retreat with the Cistercians, but he doesn't want to go. Now I've heard he's sleeping with that young woman. I don't know what went wrong."

The conversation about my nightmares wasn't happening. Instead, I saw in front of me a tired, old man whose son had slipped off the rails. We sat there in silence for a moment or two, and he finally raised his head, unspent tears glittering in his blue eyes. "You can't go back to St. Xavier's anymore. God is calling people out of that place, and you are among the first." He sighed deeply. "Eventually, we'll have to close the church out there. You need to take refuge here, in the Mother House. Don't go back there, Mary Joseph."

I slowly nodded my head in assent. Sensing that my interview was over, I rose to my feet, and the Bishop pulled himself up from his chair. He reached out a hand, and I bowed, leaning my head forward. Marking my forehead with the sign of the cross, he added, "When you are no longer going there, the bad dreams will stop." I nodded again, a tight smile on my lips. I thanked him and left the room. I felt no better for the encounter. The Bishop told me to abandon the sinking ship and save myself.

***

A feeling of groundlessness overwhelmed me. As much as the nonstop work of being a sacristan at St. Xavier's had worn me down, part of me wondered how I would define myself and my role in the CRC without it. I decided to go back to St. Xavier's one last time to clean the chapel again and to say goodbye to the place I had come to see as both a cage and a refuge. My timing was good; Thomas wasn't around that day. When I finished, I knelt in the back of the chapel, looking at the crucifix. No tears came, but I was overcome with a strange heaviness, a sadness that enveloped me in a suffocating embrace.

At home that evening, I called Sr. Catherine and told her what the Bishop had instructed me to do. I didn't refer to the nightmares, and for her part, Sr. Catherine made no comment on the situation. She told me that she would place me on the rotation of sacristans that cared for the Mother House. With that, almost ten years of my life came to a quiet, bloodless end. As the Bishop predicted, the nightmares slowly faded away.

All True Vows

One Last Encounter with Fr. Thomas

Leaving a place you've come to know well, where you've become part of the furniture, is never easy. Even when the leave-taking is part of a larger happy event, like graduation or moving out for the first time to set up a home of your own, you still experience a bit of nostalgia. At St. Xavier's, I was more or less my own boss as a sacristan. I set my own schedule, did what was necessary, and had the satisfaction of doing my job well. What I didn't miss about walking away was dealing with Thomas. Not having to respond to his mercurial demands made my life much simpler. Through the rumor gristmill that fed the CRC, I learned that the Bishop had sent Thomas to the mission house in Nevada, but apparently the couple who founded that house forced Thomas out on the grounds that he was too disruptive and too demanding. Surprise, surprise. The tiger had evidently not changed his stripes.

Somewhere within the Mother House, the Bishop had tucked Thomas away, the prodigal taken back again, probably a bit cowed for the moment and assuredly acting all penitent and selectively self-righteous. It seemed natural to me to assume Thomas was rooming somewhere in the Bishop's own house, to be near enough so he could receive regular dressing-downs.

It was a Saturday, and I was on the schedule to set up for Sunday mass at the Temple. Part of my duties were to check the chapels in all of the houses as well. I made my way over to the youth house, a recent purchase by the CRC which continued the Bishop's unofficial mission of buying up all of the available real estate in the neighborhood. The

Bishop's Aunt Jo lived in an apartment created for her on the second floor of the house, with the first floor used as both a preschool and a meeting spot for the youth group.

It was dark and quiet in the house when I entered. I turned to the chapel, located to the right of the front door, and started to clean. I dusted all of the woodwork, put out fresh candles, and changed the liturgical cover on the altar. I marked the record book with notes regarding needed supplies and gathered the dirty rags to take with me across the street. It was then that I heard a voice. "Mary Joseph, come here." Damn it! I thought. What the hell is *he* doing over here? I paused, trying to figure out a way to leave the house without having to respond to his call. But I was trapped. In order to go out the front door, I had to cross in front of the meeting room where the voice had emanated from.

I sighed, knowing I was caught. I walked out of the chapel into the outer room. Thomas lay on a couch, bundled up in a blanket. He looked peaked, wan, and sickly. I stared at him. He coughed and sniffled. I shuddered, repulsed. If he was truly sick—and I reserved judgment on that—I didn't want whatever he had. My money was on him faking it, a play for more underserved sympathy. I wasn't offering anything. He would have to make the first move.

"How are you?" he finally asked.

"Fine," I said, my voice short. I didn't ask him the same in return, but he pushed on.

"I'm sick. They thought it was bronchitis, but it's just a bad cold." He sounded peeved at the lesser of the two potential diagnoses. I didn't reply. I was providing no fuel for this fire. "Are you going to the main house?"

"Yes." He shifted under the blankets. I could see he was wearing a V-necked T-shirt, and the hair on his chest was grayer than before. His bare feet protruded from the end of the blanket, and almost certainly he was dressed only in his underwear. "Could you bring me a coffee? There's none here for me to make for myself."

The very thought of him making coffee for himself almost made me laugh. If there had been a can of coffee in the house, he would have asked me to make it for him.

I stood there, and suddenly saw him for what he was, a pathetic lump of human flesh. The man who confidently demanded conformity was gone.

"What do you want in it?" I found myself asking. I didn't know why I was going along with the request. Maybe because my natural inclination was to be kind. Maybe because I wanted to let him know he held no sway over me, that I was simply treating him as any other beggar, a work of mercy I would perform for a thirsty dog as well as for someone who thought too much of himself.

"Cream and two sugars. Thank you, Mary Joseph."

I nodded my head and turned to the door. He sighed as I left. He wanted me to ask what he was doing there, how he was doing, dole out sympathy for his plight. I had none to give. That well had dried up a long time ago.

I went to the main house and completed a few more tasks before heading to the kitchen where the coffee urn was set up. I mixed the drink and went back to the youth house.

"Thank you." He slurped the coffee. "Hey, sit down, talk to me for a while." He said this casually, as if the idea of having a chat with him was something I wanted to do.

I jingled the sacristan house keys on their ring. "No, I have work to do." I turned my back on him, left the house, and headed back across the street. I didn't look back. It was the last time I spoke to him. I heard later that he left the Priesthood and went to work for his brother doing odd jobs.

Was Thomas a manipulative bastard? Definitely. Did he believe in what he preached? Yes, I think he did, which was the most frightening thing of all. Thomas believed in a god that had set the world up to work in a certain way, an order to all things. There was only black and white, no shades of gray. In the end, the shadow within himself that he had struggled with overcame him and brought him down along with the church he pastored.

Sharon Downey

The Goose and the Gander

Work was the predominate thing in my parents' lives; you did it because you had to, not because you enjoyed it or were fulfilled by it. (You even kept working while having a heart attack.) My parents split the world into dichotomies: black and white, good and bad, and male and female. Women performed certain tasks, men did others. No mixing or matching, no crossing the line. I even remember my mother telling me that one of the women she worked with at her cleaning job had taken a "man's job" moving tables, buffing floors with an electric machine, and doing other "heavy" tasks. The male cleaning staffers hated the woman in question for taking a job they felt belonged to a man, and the women workers questioned her sanity.

I don't know why I thought things would be different in the church. The egalitarian message of Jesus, openly interacting with women, calling them to preach as well as the men, did not translate easily into the world of the CRC. Sacristans—primarily women—cleaned, ironed, decorated, and catered to men. This was the ideal. We were handmaids of the Lord—"handmaid" being a sweet way of saying housekeeper.

The CRC had a few women who were ordained as preachers and given the title of evangelists. Unlike their male counterparts, the CRC did not give them the opportunity to be in charge of an out-of-town house or lead a congregation of their own. Many of the evangelists held positions in the nursery schools found in some of the churches within the CRC. If you were a woman, you could teach little kids, but for the most part, preaching to adults was a male role.

The double standard towards women in the CRC was an ongoing occurrence, but two events stick out in my memory. Sr. Catherine had assigned me to go with Sr. Janet, an older sacristan, up to Crawford County to Blessed Sacrament church to prepare for a wedding. We worked a long, hard day, cleaning, setting up, serving the wedding ceremony, and then packing up to drive the hour and half back to the Mother House. A few weeks later, on St. Francis Day, I was in the side room off the altar at the Temple, ready to process with the Bishop. Wayne, the pastor of Blessed Sacrament, tapped me on the arm. "Thanks for coming up," he said. "You clean good." I stared at him and then simply nodded in response. Wayne's comment was the highest compliment he felt he could bestow on any woman, a job well done in the god approved sphere for her.

***

In 1997, I traveled to Hawaii with Agnes and two other friends. Agnes did much of the organizing for the trip. The CRC had sent her brother, Jerome, to the Big Island to pastor a church there. Not quite a year before our trip, Jerome had left his wife, family, and church, and moved back to the mainland. I knew that Agnes wanted to spend time with her sister-in-law Elizabeth and Elizabeth's two children. What I didn't want was to spend my vacation in the Church. By this time, I was five years into my ten-year stint as a professed. I had set limits as to what I would and would not do for the CRC. Spending my vacation cleaning a church crossed those limits.

What I didn't understand at the time was that Elizabeth, the first evangelist ever ordained by the CRC, was in charge of this tiny satellite church, and that didn't sit too well with some in authority. The scriptures regarding women keeping silent were bandied about (1 Timothy 2:12 – *I do not permit a woman to teach or to exercise authority over a man; rather, she is to keep quiet.*). No woman had ever served as a pastor of any of the CRC's churches, and there were those who didn't see any reason to start now. The decision had been made by the Mother House; the church in Kona would be closed.

The trip was a wonderful experience, with the paradise that is Hawaii evident in every turn. From the friendly greeting at the airport, complete with fragrant leis, to the exotic hula dancing and calm blue-green waters of the Pacific, Hawaii immersed us in its beauty.

Our time in church was limited to the celebration of St. Francis Day. In the tiny chapel, decorated in white and brown, Sr. Elizabeth led us in worship. Her sermon was short, with pointed humor, even a few sly remarks about a woman leading a congregation. The irony went even further, if you factored in the knowledge that her congregation was comprised of all women that morning.

There we all were, women worshipping a dead and risen god, honoring a saint who had problems with women; St. Francis did not want to accept the vocations of females and fought against it until forced by the overwhelming fervor of the potential Brides of Christ. I had heard the Bishop preach to the evangelists that they followed in the steps of Mary Magdalene, whom he called the apostle to the apostles. I suppose that after she told the rest of the boys what she saw at the tomb, Mary Magdalene was simply supposed to go back to sweeping the floors and making supper.

Later that week, before we returned home, we spent one more day with Elizabeth and her daughters at the beach. Another beautiful day closed with tears. The girls would be leaving friends they had made. Elizabeth had lost so much—her husband, her house in Pennsylvania, and now her church on the island she had made her home. Hawaii was another failed experiment for the CRC. My heart ached for Elizabeth for the church viewing her as less simply because she was a woman. It was another sign of the duality that existed in the CRC. If you didn't fit the mold, if you didn't play the role you were born into, you were removed and discarded.

All True Vows

The Mary Statue and the Green Scapular

Inana. Astarte. Demeter. Hekate. Banbha. Brid. Freya. Cerridwen. Kali. Isis. Lakshmi. Persephone. Miriam.

Humanity relegated these names to the broom closet of history—or so the men who worship the one god seem to think—left to the shadows, hidden and forgotten amidst the detritus and debris of the past. But like the moon in the sky, waxing and waning, ever changing and ever faithful, She Who Is still lives in the blood, bone, and sinew of her daughters, the children of women. In the church, I then knew her only by one name—Mary, the mother of god.

When the Temple had been renovated, a shelf had been installed between two stained-glass windows high on the wall of the balcony in which the women had been segregated from the men when this building had been a Jewish synagogue. On it was a statue of Mary as Our Lady of Fatima, dressed in white- and gold-decorated robes, a gold and bejeweled crown on her head, her feet perched on a cloud. On either side of the statue were two large candlesticks, which the sacristans had to light before every service. It became a common saying among the sacristans—"I'll go light Mary."

The statue was positioned dead center, facing the altar below. It gave Mary a bird's-eye view of the entire spectacle before her. The CRC had not created a niche on the altar for her, as in so many of the older style Roman Catholic churches. She usually stands to the right of the center altar, where the crucifix and tabernacle were kept. There was too much of the anti-Roman element in the Church, which had a deep aversion to "popery," to give her a place next to the holy of holies. I found that idea amusing. The priests, gathered in their brightly colored vestments, flung incense and holy water at the congregation and lifted the host to the sound of chiming bells. What could be more popish than all of that?

In the ritual of the mass, in the remembrance of Christ and his death, he and his angry father took center stage. The woman who might upstage them was shunted aside, cooling her heels in the balcony. I volunteered often to light Mary. I took the opportunity to whisper requests to her as I pulled the heavy candlesticks down to light them. I was my Baba's granddaughter, relying on Mary's kindness and power. I think Mary understood something about being seen as second rate, demoted, and unwanted. In another time, Mary of Nazareth would have been worshipped as a goddess. For me, she came to symbolize the Great Mother, the giver and taker of all life.

The Bishop's devotion to Mary was unabated by those of more evangelical persuasion. He decided those in Chapter had to be enrolled in the green scapular and wear it as part of our garb. The green scapular was one of many different versions of this devotion to Mary. A scapular is two pieces of embroidered fabric strung together with ribbon that you wear around your neck. One part of the scapular rests on your chest, the other on your back, representing armor—like a breastplate and a back covering—to keep you safe from attack by evil. Most of these scapulars promised entrance into heaven upon death— if you wore the scapular and shared its merits with others.

The green scapular was even more far-reaching. A simple single piece of embroidered cloth, worn around the neck to lie on the breast, this scapular didn't even have to be worn to work. You could put it in between the mattress and box spring of the bed of someone who didn't believe. If you said the words "Immaculate Heart of Mary, pray of us, now and at the hour of our death," Mary the Mother of God would pluck that person safe from the fires of hell at his or her death. Jesus, the message of salvation, the power of the cross—no need for any of that. Just put your faith in Mary, and a scrap of fabric and heaven would be yours. This was salvation by stealth, sneaky and clever, just another way around having someone to come to the altar and be saved by Christ and Christ alone. Here was Christ's meddling mother again, coming to the aid of sinners who should just repent on their own.

The Bishop preached about the scapular one Sunday at mass, and then everyone there was to come up and receive it. I was serving as a sacristan that Sunday and was one of the last to come up before him and receive the little scrap of embroidered fabric on its green ribbon. As he placed the scapular around my neck, he said to me, "My Mother smiles upon you." I thought nothing of it, assuming he pronounced this blessing with each of the scapulars. Mass ended, and the choir was singing yet another hymn when the Bishop said to the crowd, "If, when you received the scapular you heard the words, 'My Mother smiles upon you,' come forward in front of the sanctuary."

I paused in my work of tidying up in the sacristy and looked over at one of the other sacristans with a puzzled expression. "He didn't say that to everyone?" I asked.

"He didn't say it to me," she said, "and if he said it to you, you better get out there."

I shook my head in puzzlement and made my way to the door, passing Sr. Catherine, who stared at me in astonishment. I'm sure she viewed this as nothing more than my making a spectacle of myself. But what am I supposed to do, I thought, disobey? I stood at the front of the sanctuary, with about twenty or so other people, all of us looking at one another as if we had done something wrong and were about to be called out for it.

The Bishop then told all of us standing in the front to turn and face the congregation. The church was full, as it typically was on a Sunday, and I could feel the curious stares. Never one to want the spotlight, my face flushed. It was warm in the church, and I was sweating in my heavy polyester alb. "Those who are gathered in front of you have been given a gift. The Lord and his Mother have blessed them, and those whom they pray for and lay hands on will be healed. And they can pass on this gift to anyone who does not yet have the green scapular by enrolling them in it. If you need prayer, seek them out." The choir sent up a loud hymn of praise, and those of us facing the congregation drifted back to our places. After mass, I went up to the balcony to extinguish the candles near the Mary statue.

"Get me into trouble, will you?" I murmured as I reached with the extinguisher. Mary smiled her usual Mona Lisa smile.

***

Sr. Mary George, whom I considered to be among the "old guard" of the Chapter, approached me and asked that I pray for her. Her doctors had told her she needed to have a biopsy. I knew she believed wholeheartedly in whatever the Bishop said. If he had told her to paste the scapular to her forehead, she would have done so. I wanted to tell her that I couldn't do this simple act for her, that I didn't have any faith that my prayer for her would be any more efficacious than anyone else's. But I saw that she had faith, and I bowed to the strength of that faith. For a moment, I thought back to my own scare with cancer just a few years ago. I made the sign of the cross on her forehead and said quietly, "Dear Mother, heal our sister." It came out of my mouth without thought. I asked Mary for the miracle, not her son. Looking back, I realize that I was asking the Great Mother, the Universe herself, for help.

All True Vows

2000 and the Exodus

September 11, 2001 was a warm and beautiful day in Pittsburgh. I was working in my crowded cubicle when one of my co-workers announced her fiancé had called and told her about the events in New York City. As more bits of information came in, some true, much of it conjecture and rumor. By this time, I was working at a local university, and the Dean's office made the decision to let all of us go home. I had to wait until later in the day; buses heading to the parking lot where I left my car didn't begin running until after three. I made my way home on almost empty buses, the streets clear of traffic, and walked in the front door to find my brother with my then five-year-old nephew sitting the couch, the television replaying the scene of the planes ripping apart the Twin Towers over and over. I snapped at my brother and parents for allowing an impressionable toddler to watch that madness, and my father angrily shut the television off. After my brother left to pick up my sister-in-law from work, the news immediately came back on, and I made my way to my room. I couldn't stand to watch another minute of the coverage, with the endless speculation and commentary on what it all meant. It was enough to know that thousands of people had died an awful death at the hands of those who seemed to value their ideals over their own lives.

The following Sunday, a new item appeared in the corner of the altar at the Temple—a large American flag on a heavy pole topped with a golden eagle. The Bishop preached from the pulpit that we needed to pray for our country, our leaders, and for the courage it would take to repay those who had visited such terror on our shores—for they did not know Christ and so therefore were lost.

During the summer of 2000, before that horrible day, September 11, 2001, a new story was preached in the CRC. There was talk that we would all have to move to the "land," which was the shorthand name for the property of the church in Crawford County. The world as we knew it would come to a screeching halt—not because of terrorists with airplanes and suicide bombings or global warming making the oceans rise or the world economy collapsing in on itself—but because the polar magnets would switch. The North Pole and South Pole would change polarity, causing communication technology to fail; anything with a motor would cease to function, and even food in metal cans would be unfit to eat.

If anyone had had the commonsense to investigate the claims further, they would have discovered that the magnetic pole reversal is a common occurrence that happens over millennia. And while the situation has caused disturbances in the Earth's magnetic field, it has never disappeared completely. But common sense was sometimes in short supply in the CRC. Members of the congregation repeated the stories and believed them as if it were gospel. The survivalist mode took over certain groups of people. They talked about guns (we would need a security force) and the need for medicine, stockpiles of food, and housing. The CRC established a committee to task people with various jobs to obtain what we would need to survive. Everyone would work the land and live together like in a hippie commune until god called us all out to be the head, not the tail, that we were always meant to be. Our light would shine all the brighter in a world gone dark.

Like in *The Wizard of Oz*, we had a "man" behind the curtain. On the property in Crawford County, the CRC was building a "barn" that would house the summer youth camp. The new building would eliminate the need for the youth to travel to the church in Vermont for the summer youth camp, and it could also be rented out to earn money. It was a barn in name only. With bathrooms, windows, and central heating, it would make the life of any livestock housed in it pretty cushy. And of course, that barn had to be paid for. What better way to sell it than as an "ark" of refuge for all of us?

The CRC set up a call chain for alerting everyone when it was time to pack up and move to the "land." The CRC even planned a dry run of our "Exodus" for late August of 2000. I found the whole idea ridiculous. If the damn phones were not supposed to work when this magnetic pole reversal hit, what good would a call chain do? When anyone brought up the Exodus, I shook my head. "No need to call me," I said. "I won't be going." Even if something cataclysmic happened, how would I leave my family behind? I knew there was no good way to express my reservations about the whole enterprise, so I made a joke of it. I told those who asked me about it that they could stop at my house on their trek north for a drink of water and a snack.

Right before the rehearsal weekend, the Bishop canceled the whole test trip. He said god had told him it wasn't necessary. Since the situation had been resolved, the barn built and paid for, everyone dropped and forgot the whole idea.

***

September 11, 2001, reinforced an old way of thinking and being in the world for humanity. There was *us* and then there was *everyone else*. Fear was rampant. The world was mirroring what I had seen and experienced in the CRC for years; there were the chosen of god and there was everyone else. It only reinforced my decision that this was not how I wanted to live my life. I had one more year in my commitment of my professed vows. It was almost time to go.

Sharon Downey

The Letter of Letting Go

Sometimes walking away has nothing to do with weakness and everything to do with strength. We walk away not because we want others to realize our worth and value, but because we finally realize our own.
—Robert Tew

I sat at the computer and stared at the screen. I had put the obligatory heading at the top, the small cross followed below with the initials JMJ. I addressed each copy of the letter differently: one for the Bishop, one for the Elders, one for the archives. The standard greeting followed the address: "May the peace of God, the love of Christ, and the fellowship of the Holy Spirit be with you and those you love." I followed this with one sentence, one statement to sum up fifteen years of strife: "This letter comes to you to inform you that I will not be renewing my vows." I could not bring myself to use the pronoun "we" instead of "I." It would have rung hollow in my ears, a lie I wasn't ready to perpetuate again. The closing was the same on each missive: "Yours in His Service" and my religious name, Sr. Mary Joseph.

I printed the three letters out and signed each one with that name. I remembered choosing it, desperate to have the name of the Holy Family, one more constant reminder to god that he had to stick to his end of the bargain and give my family admittance into his kingdom. We were taught that, like any good Israelite wife, we took our husband's first name before our own, so each of us were really "Jesus Mary Xavier" or "Jesus Thomas Simon." I was Jesus Mary Joseph, the holy family. One of the founders of our order even expressed envy at my name, saying she wished she had thought to take it all those years ago.

I slipped the letters into envelopes and tucked them into the back of my office book, the green volume of ordinary time at the end of the liturgical year before the advent season when we used the blue bound book. I would take the three letters and drop them off in the mail slots located in what everyone called "Aunt Jo's Office," even though the elderly woman had been replaced by others in the task of secretarial work for the CRC. The letters would be opened, read, notations on a list made, and then someone would file them away in a creaking and overstuffed file cabinet. I had made my decision. I would not allow anyone to cajole, coax, or plead with me to change my mind. I would be free to make my life over.

I didn't discuss my decision with anyone except for Annie, who herself had made the same decision not to renew her vows. Her reasoning was simple; life had changed for her and the reasons and causes behind her taking vows no longer applied. As people discovered that I was not renewing, they each offered their own take on my decision. "Well, you have your parents to care for," they said. Early August of 2000 had brought for me new worries regarding my parents. My father suffered another heart attack, larger and more damaging than the one he experienced in 1977. Now seventy-five years old, his heart was severely weakened. Managing his care and assuming full control of the household financial matters took more and more of my time and energy. So it was true that my parents were getting older and frailer, but that wasn't the motivating factor behind my leaving the vowed life behind.

If taking vows meant that Christ and I were married, I knew our marriage vows were a sham. We weren't truly *together*, the big JC and me. We were like two strangers who had a nodding acquaintance, a mutual tolerance, and some shared history—nothing more. It had been an arranged marriage, or one of convenience, where he had deigned to allow me to be his wife in exchange for what favors I could derive from him being my husband. In my guilt over deceiving him, I undertook to work. I was like a struggling housewife, keeping the house spotless, the clothes cleaned and pressed, hot meals on the table, and my husband's numerous guests entertained. And between my spouse and me, there was dearth of feeling—only guilt on my part, pity on his.

One of the responses I received to my decision not to renew was actually quite sweet. A member of my Chapter class, Julie, was getting married. The sacristans held a wedding shower for her in the hall of the Temple, amidst the Halloween decorations. I sat at a table with some of the older Chapter members watching Julie open her gifts. As we tucked into the luncheon served afterwards, one of the women, Sr. John, leaned toward me. "I've heard you're not going to renew your vows, Mary Joseph. I was surprised. What made you decide not to go on?" Her kind face looked puzzled. Sr. John was the superior of the class directly ahead of mine, a warm-hearted mother and grandmother, a nurturer through and through.

Before I could open my mouth to respond to her query, Sr. Mary George butted in. "Sr. John, we are not to ask why a Chapter member is not renewing their vows. That is between them and the Lord."

I turned to Mary George, who, while a kind woman, was a stickler for rules. I knew she wanted to know why I wasn't renewing as much as Sr. John did, but she would never ask. I sighed. "Sr. Mary George," I said, "Sr. John asked the question in a spirit of love and kindness, and I'm choosing to answer her." Mary George looked as if she had swallowed a particularly sour pickle. I tried to squash the smile that rose to my lips. "Sr. John, I believe my time here is finished. Some are only called for a season; that's why our vows are not perpetual." The words slipped from my lips easily. But in my head, I was thinking, *It is time to call a spade a spade and move on.*

Sr. John smiled at me. "If you have peace in your decision, Mary Joseph, that's all that matters. Just know that you will be missed."

Many assumed that I made my decision because of the loss of St. Xavier's, but that had happened so many years before. I knew that I had moved on from it. I was bone dry, an empty well with nothing left to give and no means of finding more water within the Church. One of my fellow sacristans looked at me and said, "I just knew you wouldn't renew," as if her smug assessment of my unfitness for the continued struggle in the vowed life was a forgone conclusion. In the end, I truly didn't care what other people said or thought or believed. It was enough for me to know that the end was in sight.

A week before the renewal service, Sr. Felicity, now the Mother General of the Chapter, called me. She invited me to come to the renewal service, to receive an exit blessing from the Bishop. I was polite on the phone, letting her talk, without agreeing to the invitation. I didn't go. I wanted to slip away quietly, no questions, no whispered comments. I had no desire to look back. I was not looking to pick at my wounds. I wanted to heal.

Sharon Downey

Magic

My Baba, my mother's mother, had a faith in god that was practical and sustaining. She took at face value the doctrines and dogma of the church, but she put her own unique spin on Catholicism as well. My Baba did things like put an empty coin purse on the window ledge under a full moon so that she would never run out of money. Every Good Friday, before the noon hour, she insisted we all wash our hair. Then she would cut little snippets from our heads in the pattern of a cross while we blessed ourselves. If we didn't perform the ritual, we would suffer dire consequences. (I never learned what those consequences were.) The first person who entered our house on New Year's Day ideally should have been a dark-haired man carrying money and whiskey; otherwise, we would have lousy luck all year. When you saw a priest, you blessed yourself, not because they were holy, but because they wore cassocks—at least they used to—and a man dressed as a woman was bad luck. Novenas were powerful prayers because you recited them for nine days, which was a lucky number. And if you couldn't get a priest to hear your confession, you enumerated your sins to a bowl of soil so the earth herself would forgive you.

My time in the CRC had taught me that magical thinking, much as my grandmother had practiced, was still going on in the name of Christ. If a priest held two blessed, ribbon-entwined candles under your chin while saying the correct prayer, he would ensure that god would protect your throat from disease. Chalk blessed on the feast of the Epiphany was used to write the initials of the names of the three wise men on doorways to protect those inside. The Bishop carried relics of saints in the pockets of his robes to protect him from harm. Wayne, the pastor in Crawford County, burned blessed palm fronds from Palm Sunday during tornado warnings to keep the storm away.

After I had left Chapter, I became a religious wanderer. I had no desire to go back to the patriarchal monotheistic religions of any stripe or flavor. Like so many women before me, I had found the book *The Mists of Avalon* by Marion Zimmer Bradley to be an eye opener. It portrayed a world where women were priestesses in service to a goddess! It led me to look for other books on goddess spirituality and earth-based religions. I read the book *In the Circle Round*, by Elen Hawke, a witch living in England who practices Wicca. The book detailed instructions for honoring the Wiccan sabats and performing workings to ask for healing and other needs.

I slowly accumulated items I would need for an altar—candles of different colors for the four directions, dishes for water and salt, a feather to represent the element of air, and a homemade pentacle of tin foil. I had no athame (a ritual blade) or wand, no besom (a broom used to sweep a magical circle), or a goddess statue. I had only the bare bones of magical tools, but I had two things in abundance: audacity and need. I had the totally unfounded and uncorroborated belief that if I performed the rite as written in the book, something would happen. The phrase "as above, so below," referencing how the world of the spirit was reflected in the material world, was nothing new to me, if I had given it any thought to the concept at all.

As for my parents, they continued to attend the eleven o'clock mass on Sundays, leaving the house at exactly half past ten, as they did every week. Despite the fact that the church was five minutes from our house, my father insisted they leave thirty minutes ahead so he could get a primo parking space right in front of the church and not have to wait to exit the church's lot when the mass was over. I declined to join them, telling my mother I'd had enough church for the last fifteen years—thank you very much.

***

We had received a notice that our real estate tax assessment of our home was going to climb from the current $70,000 to over $90,000, resulting in a sizeable tax increase. The process to fight the increase meant going to the county courthouse and presenting information on houses comparable to our own and prove that the county had over-assessed our home. My mother and I had attended a meeting that gave information on how to calculate the price per square foot that the county used to assess each house. I made this a project for myself, producing a full-color binder of photos and graphs that showed our home to be worth about $66,000. While I was confident that my calculations were correct and my folder of proof would be more than sufficient evidence to have the assessment reduced, I wanted the boost of a magical working to put my request into the universe.

On a lovely summer Sunday morning, after my parents had left for church, I assembled my altar and put out a piece of gold-colored cord to bind the outcome of the spell. I cast the circle and cleansed it with the elements, using the salt, the water, the feather, and a lit votive candle. Then I asked the elements—air, fire, water, and earth—to be the guardians of my circle. To raise energy, I chanted and danced. When I felt in my body that I had made the connection to Spirit, I knotted the cord nine times. I said a chant from Elen Hawke's book and focused my intent on the cord, seeing in my mind the outcome of the hearing in our favor.

After sitting in meditation before the altar for a while, I released the guardian elements, took down the circle, and placed the cord in a container for safekeeping. I put away all of the altar tools. Moments later, my parents came home to find, rather than a practicing witch, their only daughter sitting on the couch reading a novel. My new practice, that was so natural to me it could hardly be called new, was mine, not to be shared or discussed. My years of setting up altars, of following the order of services, had made the ritual of circle casting and spell work easy and fluid for me.

The date of the assessment appeal came. My mother, father, and I trooped into the tiny office. The reviewer, a burly man too large for the small desk he occupied, paged through my binder. He complimented me on my hard work, and then looked at my father. "How about $60,000?" he asked. My parents and I were stunned; this was even lower than the amount I had calculated. My father put out his hand to the reviewer and they shook.

We expressed our thanks and left the office. At the elevator, my mother said to my father, "Well, thank your daughter for all of her efforts; otherwise, we'd be in real trouble." He looked at me and nodded his head. I really was not expecting anything from him; lowered expectations led to lowered disappointments. I was just happy that the outcome was in our favor.

My grandmother's faith had been underpinned by the ancient pagan rituals and beliefs that Christianity had coopted for itself. My own faith was now in a Divine Mystery which did not ask for blind obedience or even belief. I now worked with a power that was both immanent and transcendent, who could take the shape and form of a female, and who whispered deep in my soul, "You are enough."

Sharon Downey

Ireland and Making Peace

The woman at the travel insurance company had been brisk, but pleasant, explaining she would email me a list of items I would need to gather and provide to process my claim. In May of 2009, I was scheduled to join a tour group to see Ireland. It would be a dream trip for me to the island where my father's grandparents had come from. He had always wanted to see the land of his ancestors, but he lacked the funds, and poor health had long made it impossible for him to go.

Since January of that year, he and my family had been on a whirlwind of doctor's appointments, tests, and more doctor's appointments. His complaints of stomach distress and diarrhea, coupled with his ongoing heart issues, had ended with a colonoscopy and the diagnosis of colon cancer. The rogue cells were at either end of his colon, making the removal of only sections of it impractical for a man as sick as my father was. The doctors determined a total colectomy as the only option. My phone call to the travel insurance company had just canceled my trip.

In addition to the colon cancer, my father's heart failure was worsening. In order to give him the best chance of surviving the removal of his colon, Dad's cardiologist determined that my father needed to be admitted to the hospital. That evening, I entered my father's hospital room. His IV meds, what my brother had taken to calling "Dad's special cocktail," had been changed yet again. All of the drugs bolstered my father's weakened heart, helping to eliminate the fluid from his body that was pooling in his lower extremities. He sat in the chair beside the bed, so small and frail looking. The nurses' aide, Jason, had helped Dad get cleaned up. He sported a fresh shave.

"Well, don't you look spiffy!" I told my father. He smiled. My mother followed me, carrying the newspaper. She bent down and kissed his wide, smooth forehead.

"Can you clean my plate for me?" he asked, meaning his upper denture. I pulled open the drawer of the nightstand and removed Polident tablets and a denture cup.

"Put it in here and I'll take care of it. Do you want to brush your teeth?"

"Yeah," he said. My mother settled into a chair next to my father. He handed me the denture and I went into the bathroom. The faucet, even at full tilt, didn't give anything more than lukewarm water. I brought back a cup and put the tray table in front of Dad, with toothpaste, toothbrush, and an emesis basin.

"OK, you're all set," I told him. He started brushing his remaining teeth while my mother talked to him about the bills that had come in the mail that day. I soaked his plate in the Polident and then brushed it with a toothbrush and some paste. I kept going over it, delaying my announcement of cancelling my trip. I knew this was going to upset him. I cleared up the tray table and gave him back his plate. I sank down on the edge of his bed.

"Dad?"

"Huh?" He was still wiping his face with a towel.

"Listen to your daughter," my mother commanded him.

"I'm listening. What?"

"I cancelled my trip," I blurted out. He looked at me, then at my mother, as if trying to understand what I had just said. "I can't go until I know you are better," I pushed on. Then the awful happened. His jaw began to tremble and tears filled his eyes. In his usual fashion, he turned to my mother, the mediator.

"She has to go," he croaked, his voice thick. "I'll be OK." I leaned forward and touched his arm.

"Dad, I'm just postponing the trip. I'll get all of my money back. I bought trip insurance. And when you are better, I'll go."

He lifted his eyes and looked straight at me, something he rarely did. The same gray-blue eyes that were mine looked back at me. "What if I don't?" he asked. We had finally acknowledged the elephant in the room. All of this treatment was to allow my father to be strong enough to endure an hours-long operation to remove his cancerous colon. There were no guarantees that his heart would be ready for such an ordeal, no certainty he would survive the operation. But it was this or a slow, painful death as the cancer ate him up from the inside and his heart continued to worsen. Or as my brother had succinctly put it, "There is worse and then there is much worse."

"Can you tell the future?" I asked my father.

"We don't know what will happen," my mother said. "It's your daughter's choice to go to Ireland or not. She wants to be here. Besides, who will bring me to see you?"

"Your son," he said.

My mother huffed. I jumped in before an argument could break out. "It's all settled. I already contacted the insurance company and the tour company. Now, what you have to do," I said looking straight at my father, "is do what the doctors tell you and pee out all of this fluid." I looked at the wall, where the nursing staff kept a tally of his fluid input and output. "Tsk, tsk," I said, shaking my head. "We need more production on the output side!" I turned and smiled at both of them. My mother jumped on the bandwagon.

"Yeah, Dad, talk to those kidneys. Tell them to hurry it up!"

My father wisely decided to not press the issue further, knowing full well that he could not fight both of us.

An ambulance moved my father to Shadyside Hospital, where the cancer center was located. He had the operation to remove his colon, but he steadily declined afterwards. In addition to the heart failure, he developed atrial fibrillation, which sent his already weakened heart into dangerous rhythms. On May 4, 2009, he died alone in the early morning hours. I remember my mother asking his cold body, "Why couldn't you wait till I got here?" Even in the end, there was friction between them, and my father's non-responsiveness was the same in death as it had been in most of his life.

***

In September 2010, I set out for a two-week trip to Ireland. I had guilt about leaving my mother behind by herself. She assured me she would be fine, but her eyes told a different story. She was used to picking up the phone and calling me every day at work and having me for company every evening. I was her outlet, her friend, her confidant. I had to choose between the guilt of feeling as if I had abandoned her and the burn of resentment in not living the life I wanted to live. I chose guilt, which—as anyone raised on it, as I was, can tell you—is a heavy, large and uncoated pill to swallow.

Before joining my tour group, I made plans to visit Newgrange and Knowth, the Neolithic tombs in the Boyne valley, built almost a thousand years before the pyramids of Giza. On my first day in Ireland, I boarded a van to take me to the site. At Newgrange, our guide demonstrated how the light would enter the tomb on Winter Solstice morning. She extinguished the electric light inside the corbeled stone tomb. Even though all of us knew what she was about to do, when the utter blackness descended at the flick of the switch, we made a collective gasp. Then slowly, a stream of light came from the doorway, simulating the rising sun on Winter Solstice morning. The entire chamber filled with a warm expanse of light until the stones that lined the walls glowed. It was magical and mysterious, a moment as holy and precious to me as I had ever known in the Church.

At Knowth there was a ladder you could climb that took you to the roof of the tombs below. I carefully climbed the rungs. The fog and the rain of the early morning dissipated in the late summer sun, and the entire Boyne valley spread out before me, with lush green pastures, tiny farm buildings, and clusters of trees. The roof had loose stones, and our guide cautioned us to stay back from the edge. Someone had taken some of those loose stones and made a cairn, deliberately stacking the rocks one a top the other. Such cairns often mark the path on a trail or the spot of a grave. I remembered the Jewish custom of placing a stone on a grave marker to let the dead know you had visited.

I bent down and placed three small stones, one on top of the other, near the edge of the roof. "Dad, look," I whispered. "Isn't it beautiful here?" I turned and made a slow circle, looking around the valley. Thousands of years ago, my ancestors gathered here, struggled to build this place, worshipped their gods, and buried their dead. I picked up a small gray stone, fingered it and placed it in my pocket, a talisman to remind me of all those who had come before me. Had I made my peace with my father and my mother? With my choices? With my past? All I knew was that I was making an honest effort to do so. My narcissistic martyrdom was behind me. What lay before me was still unknown. I was on the spiral path, one that weaves in and out, on the journey home to myself.

Acknowledgments

With every work we accomplish in our lives, it is seldom that we attain our goal without help and support from others. I want to list here some of those whose help and encouragement were instrumental in making this book a reality.

To Jen Louden, teacher, author, and creator of her fabulous Taos Writer retreats, thank you for your support, encouragement, and love. This book was birthed under the New Mexico sun with your gracious help. Much love to you.

To Marianne Elliott, whose brave storytelling inspired me to write my own story. Your wait for this book is finally over.

To Tammy Roth, whose manifesting ability is breathtaking and who gave me the name of her editor, I am forever in your debt. You rock, my friend.

To Joanna Powell Colbert, creatrix of the Gaian Tarot and gifted writer—thank you for sharing your story with me in Taos and for your encouragement on this writing journey. I can't wait to see what you create next.

And to my brother, Norm, who when he read this work, responded "Wow." Thank you for always being there for me. I love you.